RECESSION-PROOF
REAL ESTATE INVESTING

RECESSION-PROOF REAL ESTATE INVESTING

HOW TO SURVIVE **(AND THRIVE!)** DURING ANY PHASE OF THE ECONOMIC CYCLE

BY J SCOTT

BiggerPockets®
PUBLISHING
Denver, Colorado

Recession Proof Real Estate Investing
J Scott
Published by BiggerPockets Publishing LLC, Denver, CO
Copyright © 2019 by ScottBuilt, LLC
All Rights Reserved.

Publisher's Cataloging-in-Publication Data
Names: Scott, J, author.
Title: Recession-proof real estate investing : how to survive (and thrive!) during any phase of the economic cycle / by J Scott.
Description: Includes bibliographical references. | Denver, CO: BiggerPockets Publishing, 2020.
Identifiers: LCCN: 2020935645 | ISBN: 9781947200395 (pbk.) | 9781947200197 (ebook)
Subjects: LCSH Real estate investing. | Personal finance. | Investments. | BISAC BUSINESS &ECONOMICS / Economic Conditions | BUSINESS & ECONOMICS / Real Estate / Buying & Selling Homes | BUSINESS & ECONOMICS / Investments & Securities / Real Estate | BUSINESS & ECONOMICS / Real Estate / General | BUSINESS & ECONOMICS / Personal Finance / Investing
Classification: LCC HD1382.5 .S385 2020 | DDC 332.63/24--dc23

Cover Design: Alicia Tatone
Cover Image: Kativ/iStock

Published in the United States of America
Printed in the USA on recycled paper
10 9 8 7 6 5 4 3 2 1

For Rookie—for 15 years, you sat by my side as I worked, keeping me company and brightening my day. This is the first project I've had to complete without you. It wasn't nearly as easy or fun.

I miss you, little girl.

J Scott

TABLE OF CONTENTS

PREFACE

The original manuscript for this book was written in 2017 and 2018 and published by BiggerPockets in 2019. At the time of its writing, the market felt like it was on the verge of change. We had seen unprecedented growth after the 2008 recession, with nearly ten years of economic stability and—for the most part—prosperity. But there were a lot of indicators that an economic slowdown was imminent, and many investors I knew were starting to consider that changes were on the horizon.

Less than a year later, the coronavirus (COVID-19) pandemic hit. At first, this seemed to be the nail in the coffin for the huge run-up of home prices and the steep gains of the stock market. And, for a few months, it was.

During the spring of 2020, property values plummeted as people were locked down in their homes. The stock market dropped 30 percent nearly overnight. Unemployment skyrocketed. If you were like me, you probably assumed that what was coming next would make the 2008 recession look mild.

Turns out, we were wrong. While there was economic fallout for many, the markets recovered quickly. And drastically.

Home prices shot up to levels we'd never seen before. The stock market rallied to recoup its losses and add another 10 to 20 percent gains. Cryptocurrencies like Bitcoin shot up five-fold in a matter of months. Millionaires—and billionaires—were made overnight.

However, as we saw leading into 2021 and 2022, every action has an equal and opposite reaction. In this case, the opposite reaction was supply shortages and crippling inflation. The availability of things like furniture, cars, baby formula, and building materials dwindled. And the price of everyday goods—from gas to food to lumber—shot through the roof. We were getting richer through our 401(k)s and investments; yet we were struggling through our everyday lives.

I'm writing this updated preface in June 2022, as I watch what may be the end of the post-COVID-19 financial frenzy. The stock market is starting to struggle. Housing inventory is up, with buyers making fewer sight-unseen offers far above asking price. Cryptocurrency is no longer the rage. And, in general, economic confidence is at a low point not seen since the beginning of the COVID-19 crisis.

If the past two years have taught me anything, it's that I can't predict what's next. Will this economic slowing lead to a recession? If so, will it be short-lived or will it rival the crash of 2008? Or, perhaps, is what I'm seeing here in June 2022 just another blip on the economic radar, and the party will continue?

If nothing else, this is a good reminder that none of us—including the most brilliant of economists—can predict what's next when it comes to the economy. Even ignoring black-swan events like the pandemic, there are simply too many variables at play for any of us to have a crystal ball to discern where housing prices, or the stock market, or cryptocurrency, or any type of investment is likely to be months or years from now.

It's also a good reminder that economic shifts don't just happen randomly. Cause and effect is at play. The better we are at knowing where to look, and what to look for, the better we will be at determining when a shift may be coming, and in which direction. Nobody could have predicted exactly when and how COVID-19 would sweep the planet; but, given the extent of the global challenges created by the pandemic, and given the financial response to COVID-19 by governments around the world, it wasn't difficult to predict some of the financial fallout. Perhaps not enough to know exactly where the economy is headed, but at least enough to give smart investors an edge—and even a head start.

For example, between supply chain disruptions and the printing of trillions of dollars, it wasn't a stretch to assume that there would be some inflation. And with eighteen months of lockdowns, it isn't much of a surprise that attitudes about remote work have changed. Many investors have been able to leverage their predictions of these two outcomes to generate a lot of money over the past year.

Again, it's not about reading the tea leaves and knowing exactly what's going to happen. It's about exploiting small pieces of information to get an investing edge. It's about seeing the trends before others do to get a head start. It's about being flexible in your investing efforts so that you can pivot and change strategy when you see an opportunity (or a potential pitfall).

As you read this book, keep in mind that economics is not like physics—there are no universal laws that define how markets, people, or even governments must act and react. While we talk about the history of the economy in this country, remember that history is a great predictor of the future, but it's not a crystal ball. During this economic crisis, this economic cycle, and all future economic cycles, it's possible that we will see action and reaction that has never been seen before.

As an investor, you must also be a student of economics. And as a student of economics, you must be constantly willing to take in new information, add it to the economic models in your head, and then use those models to spit out the best information possible. While others are simply being dragged along by economic news and events, those who understand the basic concepts behind how things work will be best positioned to lead the pack, make good decisions, and survive (and thrive) financially.

Like I said, I don't know if what we're seeing today is the beginning of the next recession or, if so, how bad that recession will be. (As you'll learn from reading this book, not all recessions are like the 2008 crash.) However, even if this is not the beginning of the next recession, sooner or later, it will come. While we'll have no control over it, we can control how we react to it and how we modify our businesses and investments to take advantage of a changing economic reality and the twists and turns that come with it.

While it's the eventual downturn in the real estate market cycle that led me to write this book, my goal isn't just to teach you how to make money in a down market. It's to teach you how to make money at almost any point in the economic cycle.

In fact, as you'll learn, when it comes to real estate investing, opportunities are almost always available. You just have to know where to look. It doesn't matter if you're reading this while we're at the top of a hot market, during a market downturn, or at the start of the next market cycle.

Opportunities abound, and I will teach you how to find them.

Before I discuss the specific strategies and tactics you should be using at various points in the economic cycle, it's important that you understand how the cycle works, what drives it, what impacts it, and how it affects us as real estate investors. The economy is ever-changing, and I can't just give you a bulleted list of steps to master it: You need to understand why the economy does what it does. Once you have that foundation, not only will the strategies and tactics I discuss make more sense but you'll also have the tools you need to deviate and modify those strategies and tactics, based on unique situations you're sure to encounter in the future.

In this book, I'm going to provide that foundation. Then I will build on that foundation. I'll teach you how you can profit from real estate during the various parts of the economic cycle, as well as how you can recognize shifts in the market and prepare your investing business for upcoming market conditions.

While much of your competition will change or even go away as the market changes, with the knowledge I'll provide, you'll be able to build a real estate business that will not only survive the shifts but also *thrive*.

Have any more questions that I don't cover in this book? Or maybe you just want to keep the conversation going? Please hop onto the forums on BiggerPockets.com and connect with other like-minded real estate investors!

NOTE

I want to provide one very important warning before you continue reading:

Much of the information provided in this book is based purely on my opinion, my experience, and my investing style, as well as on historical trends and even some gross speculation.

In my experience, even successful investors will disagree on some of the advice and ideas I lay out. In many cases, differing opinions can both be correct; or both can be wrong. It all depends on the specific circumstances.

There will be exceptions to all the rules I discuss. Some might be small exceptions based on your personal situation and some might be large exceptions—for example, when the market doesn't respond in ways that it has historically. And with the current uncertainty related to health, political, and economic events, that holds even more true today than any time in recent memory.

Please do NOT rely on any information in this book to make specific investing decisions. Instead, use the information contained herein to better understand the market, the economic cycle, and how best to leverage them to build a solid, low-risk portfolio.

As always, you understand your situation, goals, limitations, priorities, and investments better than anyone, so if anything in this book contradicts your beliefs, consider that what I recommend may not be right for you.

CHAPTER 1

INTRODUCTION

In May 2008, my family and I moved to Atlanta, Georgia. Driving through the city and surrounding counties, we couldn't pass three houses without seeing a "for sale" sign in a yard or a foreclosure notice taped to a front door.

To say Atlanta had been devastated by the 2007 housing crash would be an understatement. It was one of the hardest hit markets in the United States, with housing values in some areas as low as 30 percent of what they'd been two years earlier. Foreclosure rates in Georgia were up 44 percent from 2007 and 117 percent from 2006.

And Georgia wasn't alone.

Nationwide, foreclosure filings increased by more than 81 percent in 2008, with more than 800,000 families losing their homes. And that trend continued for the next two years. From 2009 through 2010, about 45 percent of existing home sales in the United States were REOs (real estate owned) or short sales.

As we drove through the neighborhoods near our house, we couldn't understand why investors weren't taking advantage of the reduced prices and buying up the distressed properties. I started attending some local real estate meetups to see what was going on. The only information I could get from the two or three investors who attended—down from hundreds just a year earlier—was that they were too scared to buy. They were worried prices would continue to drop, and they wouldn't be able to resell their investments. In other words, these investors were passing up potential deals-of-a-lifetime because they didn't have confidence in their exit strategy.

These investors were waiting for the "perfect" time to jump back into the market. They didn't understand the real estate market works in cycles just like the broader economy—with upswings and downturns—and that there is never a perfect time. Instead, they should have been creating an investment strategy that worked across the full cycle.

This is what we do, and hopefully after reading this book, what you will do as well.

Don't Fear Change, Embrace It

Change is inevitable. And you can respond to it in one of two ways:

- You can embrace it, modify your investment strategy around it, and reap the benefits from the opportunities that present themselves.
- Or you can fear it, refuse to adapt, miss out on the opportunities that come your way, watch your profits shrink, and potentially lose money.

Successful investors are flexible. They understand that to succeed they need to be prepared to take advantage of the opportunities that come their way—whether it's during an upswing, a down market, or an inflection point (more on that later). It doesn't matter if you're just getting started or you're a seasoned veteran, there are ways to make money during every phase of the real estate cycle. But to do so, you need to have a strategy to handle changing market conditions, which is what my wife and I have done over the last decade.

When Carol and I started our real estate investment business in 2008, the housing crisis was at its worst, and the foreclosure rate was the highest it had been in modern history. As flippers, that worked to our advantage. To find our next great investment opportunity, pretty much all we had to do was choose a random home from a list of foreclosures available for sale by the banks (also known as REOs). For the first couple of years we were in business, we only bought REOs because there were so many, and nearly all of them were good investments.

But in 2010, Carol started to notice a decline in the number of foreclosures on the market. She realized if we wanted to keep our inventory pipeline full, we'd need to start looking for different types of investments by the following year. She'd heard that some real estate agents were focused on short sales, where lenders were giving sellers permission to sell their properties for less than what they owed on their loans. These types of sales were becoming more and more popular, so we decided to start shifting our buying strategy to take advantage of the increasing supply of short sales on the market.

Within a year, REOs dried up in our area, but short sales were taking off. Because we'd started building our short-sale pipeline quickly after the real estate market began to shift, we were better positioned than most investors to take advantage of this new trend in acquiring investment property.

Fast-forward two years, and Carol again recognized a change in the market. She realized banks were getting more conservative in their approvals of short sales, and suggested we find a new strategy for acquiring deals because she didn't believe short sales were going to be a viable option for much longer.

Around that time—2013 or so—I noticed builders were starting to sell off some of their excess lot inventory. These were empty lots in newly developed subdivisions that weren't as optimal as the rest of the lots and didn't have the same level of profit potential. But these lots were perfect for investors looking to build spec houses (being sold for a profit as-is or with minimal changes), which is something we wanted to pursue.

In addition, as the market started improving, we began to see opportunities to buy older homes on "infill" lots. The existing structures could be knocked down and replaced with new construction spec homes. For the next several years, building new construction spec houses was our niche. Because we saw the opportunity before many other investors, we were able to capitalize on our ability to change direction quickly and efficiently.

We continue to do so today. As I've already mentioned, COVID-19 and its economic aftermath have brought about macroeconomic changes that nobody could have predicted. It's simply another great reminder that flexibility as an investor is paramount, and without the ability to shift focus, change strategy, and adapt to an ever-changing landscape, investing success is not only not guaranteed—it is unlikely.

Whatever economic conditions are on the horizon will undoubtedly cause uncertainty and change. But history has shown us that even those changes will likely be short-lived. The investing landscape will continue to evolve, and we must evolve with it.

The goal of this book is to help you prepare for the imminent changes that will occur throughout the next economic cycle and future cycles. If you're an experienced investor who's been through a full economic cycle, you're probably already familiar with many of the concepts I'm going to discuss.

But if you're experiencing part of the cycle for the first time, understanding and applying the techniques in this book will help you earn more in any part of the real estate cycle. And it will help prevent you from getting blindsided by changes in the market.

Transactions, Markets, Economies, and Cycles

I'm sure you've heard each of these words before and you no doubt have a good idea what they mean. But I'll be using these terms *a lot* in this book, and I want to be certain that we all agree on how they are being used.

A **transaction** is simply an exchange between two people. We live in a transactional world, especially when it comes to financial transactions. Every day, billions of times per day, transactions take place between buyers and sellers. Buyers give money in the form of cash or credit to sellers, who in return for that money provide a specific good or a service to the buyer.

For example, I might give money to a restaurant for food. I might give money to a car dealership for a new car. You gave me money in return for this book! Each of those billions of transactions is based around many thousand different good and services.

If you aggregate of the transactions around one specific good or service, that's called a **market**. In other words, the automobile market is simply the sum of all of the transactions that involve automobiles. The gold market is all the transactions that involve buying and selling gold. And, as you can probably guess, the real estate market is simply all the transactions that involve real estate.

There are thousands of these markets, and when you put them all together, you get an **economy**. To put it simply, an economy is made up of thousands of markets, which in turn are made up of billions of transactions. When we talk about the economy, we are simply talking about the sum all of those transactions within all the markets within it.

As you might expect, the number of transactions and the size of transactions that take place every day across all markets isn't always going to stay the same. There will be months and years where there are more transactions and bigger transactions; when this is the case, there's lot of cash flowing through the markets, and we typically refer to the economy as *strong*.

There will be other times when there are fewer transactions and smaller transactions taking place over months or years. During these periods, there is less money flowing through the markets, and we typically refer to the economy as *weak*.

Historically, we've found that there are some well-defined factors that need to come together to generate a strong economy. Then, after some period of time, those same factors that led to the strong economy will cause problems that weaken the economy. Eventually, those same factors lead to the economy getting strong again.

This pattern of strong economy leading to a weak economy leading back to a strong economy is called a *cycle*.

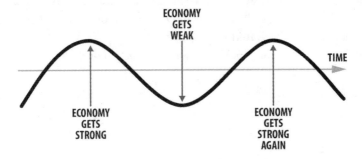

To summarize the relationship of these four concepts:
Markets—including the real estate market—are made up of billions of transactions. Those markets comprise the overall economy. And the economy goes up and down in cycles over the period of years and decades.

Common and Historical Economic Cycles

Economic cycles are not new. Experts have been tracking them for more than a century and a half. Unfortunately, those same experts — even the most respected ones—disagree over how long a cycle lasts and when we can expect a change in the current one.

Just take a look at the headlines on any given day and you can likely find one expert predicting strong economic growth for the next two to three years, while another says we're headed for a recession any day now. Another may even contend that an economic downturn started months ago.

Sometimes the experts are right and sometimes they're wrong. But two things you can count on are that no part of a cycle lasts forever, and every cycle will eventually repeat.

Changes to economic policy, tax policy, and the way businesses operate may impact the length and magnitude of our economic cycles. However, it's reasonable to assume the markets and broader economy will continue to fluctuate in response to macro- and micro-economic factors just as they have throughout history. In other words, while it may be tempting to say,

"This time is different!" history tells us that things are rarely different. The details may change, but every economic cycle is going to feel familiar and every cycle will give us—and take from us—financial opportunities.

Before we continue, it's important to point out that the cycles we'll talk about in the rest of this section (and throughout much of the book) are *national* cycles. That's not to say these cycles don't exist independently at the local level as well. They do. But keep in mind that what we discuss in the following paragraphs and chapters may not align perfectly with the cycles you've seen in your local market.

Though, for many of you, I bet it will be pretty close.

CHAPTER 2

WHAT DRIVES CYCLES

We discussed in the previous chapter that our economy moves in cycles. And it's not just one cycle at play. There are many interrelated cycles, and the interaction of these cycles is what drives the length and magnitude of the uptrends and downtrends we see in our economy.

In this chapter I want to discuss three of the cycles that have the biggest impact on our lives as both consumers and investors. While these aren't the only cycles that exist in our economy, understanding these three big ones will help you better understand why we see the economic ups and downs that are so prevalent.

The Business Cycle

The first cycle I want to discuss is perhaps the most commonly discussed and most recognized. It's called the *business cycle*. Because the business cycle occurs more often than other cycles, and tends to affect all parts of the economy, Americans are more attuned to the ups and downs caused by this cycle than all the other cycles put together.

The business cycle is driven by interaction between two main forces: inflation and interest rates. It's imperative that you understand how and why these forces work the way they do, as that's the basis for the rest of this book and for your entire investing strategy.

With that said, let's a look at how inflation and interest rates drive the business cycle.

Imagine a point in the economic cycle where the economy has emerged from a recent recession and is now chugging along well. This might correlate to what we saw back in 2002 or 2012. Now that the recession has passed, businesses are starting to generate profits again and they're hiring more workers. With all the hiring across the nation, the unemployment rate is finally leveling off and starting to drop, and people are getting back to work.

Now that many Americans are once again gainfully employed, they are starting to spend more money. They're going out to eat, they're buying new cars, and they're buying clothes. All this spending is good for businesses— they're now selling more products and services, increasing production and making more money.

As business owners start to earn more, they'll pass some of these profits onto their employees in the form of increased wages and bonuses. Employees are also consumers, and when employees earn more money, they spend more money. We're seeing a snowball effect: Increased business profits lead to increased employee wages, leading to increased spending, leading to even high business profits.

Over time, businesses hire more workers, unemployment numbers drop, and consumer confidence in the economy increases. We're once again in an economic boom, and evidence is everywhere. Tourism is booming, the stock market is going up, real estate values are going up, and investors are getting confident again.

Eventually, things are so good for the average American that demand for products and services starts to outpace the ability of businesses to produce those goods and services. Car manufacturers can't build cars fast enough. Home builders can't build homes fast enough. Electronics manufacturers can't build enough TVs or toys.

To keep up with all the demand, businesses need to hire more workers. Unfortunately, thanks to the low unemployment rate created by the strong economy, there aren't many new workers to hire. Businesses must increase their wages to get retired workers back into the workforce and to entice workers to leave other jobs and work for them.

At the same time, to ramp up production with all these new employees, businesses need to buy more equipment and build more factories. These things aren't free, and the cost of this new equipment and new factories will eat into business profits.

This quick and steep increase in wages and production costs gets passed onto consumers. Businesses owners will increase the prices of their goods and services in order to maintain profits.

The term we use for an increase in the price of goods and services is *inflation.*

Inflation is a positive sign of a growing economy, but it's also a drag on economic growth. When goods and services cost more, consumers' money doesn't go as far, leading many consumers to either spend less or use credit cards and loans to finance their purchases.

The government knows that too much inflation isn't good. In fact, runaway inflation is such a risk to consumers and the economy that it's at this point when the government will step in and start taking action.

To combat inflation, the government needs to encourage Americans to spend less money—at least for brief period of time. This will give businesses a chance to catch up on production and get ahead of consumer demand. Which should slow down inflation.

And this is where the Federal Reserve comes in...

The Federal Reserve

Sometimes called the Fed, it was created by Congress and its goal is to oversee and regulate the United States financial system. It's the one organization that can manipulate the economy from the inside.

They have two ways to do this:
First, the Fed controls the money supply. They don't print money—that's the Department of Treasury's job—but it's the Fed that decides how and when to release it into the economy. We'll talk more about this in just a moment.

Second, the Fed controls interest rates, and can raise or lower interest rates as they see fit. It's this power to affect interest rates that the Fed most often uses to manipulate the economy.

To understand how the Fed uses interest rates to manipulate the economy, we first must understand what interest rates are and how they work. Interest rates reflect the rate at which money can be loaned and borrowed. Any time money is borrowed, the borrower must pay back the amount borrowed, plus a little more. This "little more" is the lender's profit and is referred to as interest.

When interest rates are low, borrowers only need to pay back a little extra on top of what they borrowed. But when interest rates are high, borrowers must pay back much more on top of what was borrowed, which reduces their spending power on other goods and services.

By controlling interest rates, the Fed has the ability to decide whether it's cheap or expensive to borrow money.

Interest rates also come into play when saving. Low interest rates mean that when you stick your money in a savings accounts, certificates of deposit, or U.S. bonds, you don't earn very much in interest. But when interest rates are high, saving money is more lucrative.

By controlling interest rates, the Fed has the ability to decide whether it's lucrative to save money; if not, Americans will tend to spend instead.

When inflation starts to take hold, the Fed will step in and raise interest rates. Higher interest rates will have two major effects:

1. It will encourage consumers to spend less and save more—remember, higher interest rates mean higher returns from savings accounts, certificates of deposit, and bonds.
2. It will decrease consumers' abilities to borrow money—remember, higher interest rates mean higher borrowing costs.

When Americans spend less and can't borrow as much, inflation starts to slow.

Unfortunately, this reduced spending leads to a slowing in the overall economy as well. This will lead to businesses laying off workers they recently hired. To avoid losing their jobs altogether, some workers are forced to accept lower pay and fewer hours. Remember, employees are also consumers, so when employees are laid off and their wages are cut, they have less money to spend, and repaying their existing debts becomes more difficult.

At this point, we see another snowball effect: decreased business profits lead to decreased employee wages, leading to decreased spending, leading to even lower business profits.

We refer to this as economic contraction. Unemployment increases, consumers default on their mortgage and credit card payments, bankruptcies increase, and businesses are forced to downsize, or worse, close down. Depending on how severe the downturn is, the result may be a recession—and in some cases, even a depression, which is a long-lasting economic spiral.

Eventually, the government steps in again.

This time, the Fed decreases interest rates to encourage consumers to stop saving, help businesses borrow more and cheaper money, and stimulate consumer spending. But, speeding up the economy is more difficult than slowing it down. And while raising interest rates is enough to slow economic growth and curb inflation, lowering interest rates isn't always enough to get things moving again, especially during a really bad recessionary period.

Luckily, as we mentioned earlier, the Fed has one other option they can use to manipulate the economy—they control the money supply. It's during a severe economic downturn that the Fed can use their control over the amount of money flowing through the economy to spur additional growth and get things moving again. Specifically, the Fed can "print money," increasing the amount of capital flowing through the economy and providing the funds businesses and average consumers need to keep spending and helping the recovery.

This emergency printing of money is often referred to as Quantitative Easing (or QE). Technically speaking, the Fed doesn't actually print new currency—the term "printing money" is more conceptual than literal. Instead, the Fed gives money in the form of electronic currency credits to some of the largest banks in the country—the banks can then use this new money to loan to businesses and consumers, spreading that money throughout the economy and (hopefully) spurring economic growth.

Now, the Fed doesn't give this money for free. It actually trades these currency credits for real assets, like government bonds. The goal is that once the economy gets back on track, the Fed will reverse the trade, giving the banks back their government bonds and then removing the newly created currency from the money supply. This is important because having too much money in the money supply means that people have way too much money to spend, which can lead to inflation.

This is why we often talk QE being risky to the economy—the extra money spurs growth, but if the Fed isn't careful, it can lead to inflation, which hurts consumers. But, it's sometimes a risk the Fed is willing to take to get Americans borrowing and spending again, and get the economy back on track.

Assuming this lowering of interest rates and printing of money works, borrowing and spending will increase, the economy will begin to grow, and the cycle begins again.

As you can see, while our economy is an extraordinarily complex ecosystem, the most common economic cycles we see are due to a relatively simple pattern:

- A strong economy leads to inflation;
- Inflation leads to the government raising interest rates;
- Increased interest rates slow the economy, leading to recession;
- A recession leads the government to lower interest rates.

In visual form, a typical business cycle might look like this:

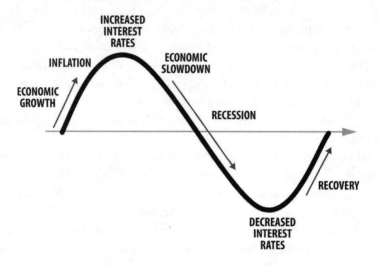

The Long-Term Debt Cycle

While the business cycle may be the one most Americans are familiar with, it's not necessarily the one that can have the greatest impact on the economy. Another cycle—some economists call it the long-term debt cycle—is a much longer cycle that impacts our economy much less often than the business cycle. But when it does, it can derail things for decades at a time. In fact, it was the long-term debt cycle that likely drove the Great Depression of the 1930s.

The long-term debt cycle exists because of a quirk in the business cycle. Each business cycle ends at a point a little bit higher than the previous one. In other words, each cycle sees a bit more economic growth than economic contraction.

Instead of two back-to-back business cycles looking like this:

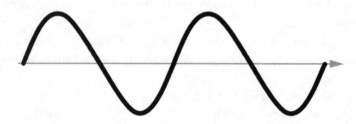

It actually looks more like this:

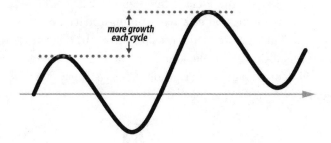

Unfortunately, what we're seeing in that graph above is not just an increase in economic growth from cycle to cycle. More economic growth means the ability to accumulate more debt, so it's also an increase in total debt from cycle to cycle:

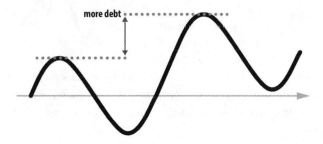

Over many business cycles—and many decades—the economy continues to expand, and so does the total debt being carried by consumers and businesses:

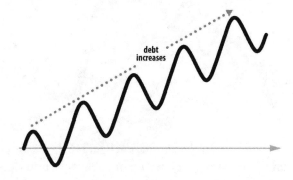

After many decades of these short-term cycles, we eventually reach a point where the total debt hits a peak and is too much for the average consumer or business to handle. The result is a much bigger downturn than what we experience with the average business cycle.

This bigger downturn is called a *deleveraging* and it ends in a substantial, long-term recession—or even a depression. After the deleveraging, debt is finally back to sustainable levels, and over many more business cycles we can start digging ourselves out of the hole. This recovery can take upwards of 20-30 years.

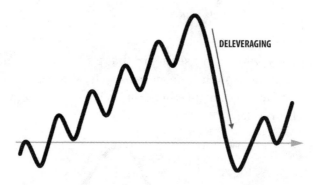

You'll notice that this long series of business cycles rising, falling, and then recovering again consists of a similar pattern to what we see in a single business cycle. But this cycle takes place over many decades, typically lasting anywhere from 50-100 years.

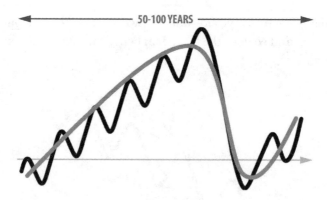

A lot of people believe that the 2008 Great Recession was the deleveraging that was part of the most recent long-term debt cycle, and that we're now in the recovery phase of this long cycle. And, if you assume that the Great Depression of the 1930s was the last deleveraging, the timing works out pretty well since 2008 was about 75 years after the Great Depression.

But there is reason to believe that the 2008 downturn wasn't the worst of it. First, the recovery we've seen in the past decade has been much quicker than what we'd typically see in a deleveraging—if this had been an actual deleveraging, it's unlikely we would have seen the recovery we've seen in the past decade.

More importantly, if you look at the nation's long-term debt trajectory, it doesn't appear that 2008 took much of a bite out of the nation's total consumer debt:

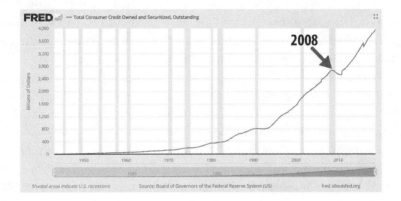

Whether 2008 was the big downturn we should expect to see in the next 50-100 years, or whether another massive downturn is coming in the near future, we don't know. But understanding how the long-term debt cycle works and understanding that large-scale recessions and even depressions are a natural part of our economy will help you keep perspective as you make your long-term investing decisions.

The Real Estate Cycle

There's one more cycle I want to discuss before we move on, as this one directly affects real estate investors. It's a cycle that some economists refer to as the *real estate cycle*.

Back in the late 19th century, an American economist named Henry George was the first to write about why we have a cyclical economy. Unlike today's economists who attribute cycles to inflation and interest rates, George believed that land speculation was the driving force behind the cycles we see.

Here is George's theory on how land speculation caused the boom/bust cycle we see in the economy:

First, we start with the fact that land has a fixed supply; we can't make more of it. In economics, we refer to this as *inelastic supply*. When something has inelastic supply, if demand for that thing increases, so does the price. When the demand for land increases, the price of land increases.

Next, we assume that in most cases developers purchase land to develop today and resell in the near future. The prices developers are willing to pay for raw land reflect what the developers can sell the property for in a year or two if they start developing it now.

But during an economic boom, investors (people like you and me) will start to buy land on speculation—in other words, not to develop now, but to hold in the hopes that the price will increase in the future. This speculation buying pushes land prices beyond the point where developers can make a profit, so developers are forced to stop buying.

When they stop buying, they stop building. And when developers stop building, this causes an economic ripple throughout the economy, hurting industries such as construction, heavy equipment, and building material manufacturing. This results in an economic recession, especially in those industries.

Eventually, speculators realize that they won't be able to make money on their land purchases, and they start selling off their inventory at reduced prices, spurring developers back into action. Developers start building again, manufacturers start selling again, and the whole cycle repeats.

This is what that looks like:

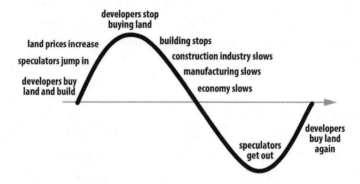

Over the past 160 years, this real estate cycle has been very consistent. It doesn't occur as often as the business cycle; instead, this cycle is on its own timetable. It occurs about every 18 years. And with the exception of several decades after the Great Depression, this 18-year cycle has been remarkably consistent, producing downturns in the real estate market independent of the business cycle downturns.

Putting the Cycles Together

We've now talked about three different cycles—the business cycle, the long-term debt cycle, and the real estate cycle. While each of these cycles will impact real estate investors and the real estate market, for the rest of this book I'm going to focus on the business cycle.

I'm going to assume that the real estate market will ebb and flow within this cycle. When we're in the growth part of the business cycle and the economy is strong, I will assume that real estate is strong with it; and when we're in the contraction part of the business cycle, heading into a recession, I will assume that real estate will get dragged along with it.

You might be wondering why I'm going to focus on the business cycle when the other two cycles also affect the real estate market. The answer is twofold:

1. The business cycle happens much more often than the other two cycles;
2. The business cycle tends to have a greater impact on the real estate market than the other two cycles

Just because I'll be focusing on the business cycle doesn't mean that you should ignore the impact of these other cycles. Especially when the downturn from two or more of these cycles coincides.

When the downturn from two or more of these cycles hits at the same time, we tend to see a much larger recession than is typical. This is likely what happened in 2008.

The business cycle was due for a downturn. The real estate cycle was due for a downturn. And some say the long-term debt cycle was due for a downturn. And because the downturn from multiple cycles coincided, the 2008 recession was a big one!

Here's something to keep in mind: If the real estate cycle saw a downturn in 2008 and typically cycles every 18 years, that means we should expect to see another dip in the real estate cycle sometime around 2026. That could be a minor real estate downturn or, if it coincides with another business cycle downturn, it could be much worse.

We won't know for sure until it gets closer, or perhaps until it's already here. Unfortunately, predicting every change in the market is impossible, which is why it's so important to be able to recognize the signs that the market is changing—we'll discuss this in detail later in the book.

CHAPTER 3

ECONOMIC SHIFTS: A CASE STUDY

In Chapter 2, we talked about the role of the Federal Reserve in keeping the economy on track. And while we made it seem like the Fed has a straightforward job, in reality, there's a lot of nuance and guesswork that goes into driving the economy forward without crashing.

Thanks to the current (mid-2022) economic situation, we have a great case study around the complexities of economic shifts and a great example of the difficult position the Fed can find itself in trying to avoid catastrophe.

I'm specifically referring to the high level of inflation we're experiencing, both in the U.S. and worldwide, and what is being done—and will likely have to continue being done—to tackle it.

We discussed earlier that it's typical to see inflation rise after an economic boom; however, what we started to see in 2021 was inflation outside what most economists consider normal or good for the economy. The Fed typically targets about 2 to 3 percent inflation per year, but the U.S. was reaching inflation levels above 8 percent by the spring of 2022.

Let's step back and talk about how we got to this point, as well as the challenge the government is facing to fix it (hopefully without creating more problems).

COVID-19 hit in March 2020. The economy ground to a halt, and it looked like we were on the verge of an economic depression. So, as is their job, the Fed stepped in to avoid economic catastrophe. I'm not going to argue that the government or the Fed made all the right decisions during this time, but the reality is that the country was in crisis mode, and extreme action was better than no action.

As a reminder, the Fed has two resources at its disposal to control the economy: setting target interest rates and printing money. In 2020, it relied heavily on both of those.

Shortly after COVID-19 hit, the Fed dropped interest rates to near zero percent. This did two things: It encouraged spending (as credit was now cheaper), and it discouraged saving (as bank accounts were essentially paying no interest on deposits).

Additionally, the Fed started to "print money." Now, the Fed doesn't really print money. But it can direct the Treasury Department to print money and then use this newly created currency to start buying things up, putting new money into the economy and spurring growth.

Between 2020 and 2021, the Fed increased the U.S. money supply by over $6 trillion, a nearly 40 percent increase. In other words, 40 percent of all money circulating through our economy was created in under 24 months.

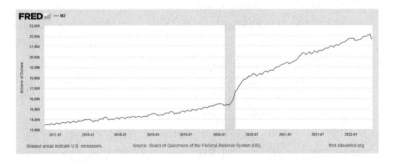

Unsurprisingly, this did the trick. Between lowering rates and flooding the market with cash, the Fed stimulated tremendous growth. In fact, it stimulated too much growth—driving up housing values, driving up the stock market, driving up other assets like cryptocurrency, and ultimately driving up the cost of everyday goods and services.

Inflation!

Most people who understand economics wouldn't be surprised to hear that all this money flooding the economy would lead to inflation. In fact, just from reading Chapter 2 of this book, you know enough to understand how growth and spending lead to price increases.

However, *a lot* of people were surprised to see inflation spike so quickly and so dramatically in such a short period. Remember, the Fed lowered interest rates and flooded the economy with money after 2008 as well, but we hardly saw inflation over the next decade. What was different this time around?

Why Was This Time Different?

Why was inflation at 2 percent for much of the decade after the Great Recession, and yet it hit 8 percent after the latest round of interest rate drops and money printing? The Fed reacted with the exact same tools in both situations. So what made inflation so much worse this time around?

Two forces drive inflation: supply and demand.

On the supply side, when the supply of goods and services is low, prices go up. Consumers are fighting over a small number of products, and the sellers of those products recognize that they can raise prices to force competitive buyers to pay more.

On the demand side, when demand for goods and services goes up, so do prices. When millions of people are competing to buy a limited number of products, sellers again recognize their position of strength and raise prices, forcing buyers to compete and pay more.

Thanks to the pandemic, we saw inflationary pressure from both sides. Due to global shutdowns, many bankrupted small businesses, tumult in raw material and transportation pipelines, and a host of other things, supply chains were—and continue to be—a global mess. In 2022, many feel that the worst of the pandemic is behind them and things are approaching normality, so there shouldn't be any more supply chain issues. Right?

Wrong. The United States is a very consumer-centric nation, not a producer-centric nation. We import stuff; we don't produce stuff. Therefore, it didn't matter what we saw in this country in terms of shutdowns and businesses operating. What mattered was what we saw in the countries we import most of our goods from. And in those countries, in 2022, there were still significant lockdowns, as well as war and political unrest.

Shipping logistics were still recovering, energy prices were sky high, chip manufacturing slowed, and global labor faced shortages. Long story short, while the major COVID-19 concerns may have seemed in the rearview, *supply was still constrained.* This was driving prices up.

It was also only half the story. There were also tremendous inflationary pressures on the demand side; demand for everything from commodities to hard assets increased.

Where was all this demand coming from? It came from people, companies, and institutions spending the trillions of dollars that were created and flooded into the market during the pandemic.

But that still doesn't answer the question: Why did we see all this demand post-shutdown when we didn't see it after 2008?

The answer is how the Fed put all this excess capital into the economy.

In 2008, the trillions of dollars created were put indirectly into the economy. The money was mostly given to the banks, allowing them to open their lending to businesses and consumers. That allowed all the extra money to slowly trickle into the economy over the course of months and years. In fact, much of that money never even made it into the economy, instead staying in bank reserves and being loaned back to the government over the next decade.

But COVID-19 was an even more acute event than the 2008 crisis, and trickling money into the economy through the banks wasn't an option. This time around, the Fed needed to get the money out there much more quickly.

The Fed pumped much of those trillions of dollars into the heart of the economy—buying stocks and bonds of American businesses, handing small businesses cash through PPP loans, and sending thousands of dollars directly to Americans.

This direct injection of capital was effective—people had direct access to the cash, without having to work through banks. But this direct cash injection into the heart of the economy caused the heart to beat faster. And that, to continue this analogy, caused our blood pressure to rise.

That high blood pressure was inflation. The dollars flowing directly into the economy led to out-of-control spending by individuals and companies alike, driving up the prices of goods, services, and investment assets. The Fed was successful at avoiding economic collapse. But it over-corrected and didn't let off the gas soon enough. Inflation got out of control.

Fixing a Tough Problem

The Fed now had to fix the problem it created.

As you know from reading this book, the best way to reduce inflation is to raise interest rates. So, in early 2022, the Fed started doing just that. In fact, it indicated that it would raise rates up to nine times in 2022 alone.

As of this writing, we've seen three of those rate hikes, but there are likely more to come. How many more? Nobody knows. Including the Fed!

While it may sound counterintuitive, even the Fed doesn't know exactly what it will take to fix the inflation problem. Raising interest rates is the solution; but how high do interest rates need to go to calm inflation?

While we don't know the exact answer, here is what we do know.

Conventional wisdom says that to reduce inflation, the federal funds interest rate must be higher than the inflation rate. This is because people need to know that they are not losing value by keeping cash, and rates higher than inflation allow people to not lose money by saving.

Interest rates are currently at about 1 percent. Inflation is currently at about 8 percent, according to the government. Does this mean we need to raise interest rates to 8 percent to curb inflation?

Fortunately, that's probably not the case. As rates start to rise, inflation starts to subside. Rates go up while inflation comes down. There will be a point of equalization somewhere between the current 1 percent interest rate and the 8 percent inflation rate where the two cross and inflation drops below interest rates.

Unfortunately, nobody—including the Fed—knows where this equilibrium point is. It may be that raising rates to 2 percent is enough to drop inflation back to 2 percent, a number we should all be comfortable with. But it's also possible that we may need to raise rates to 4 percent, 5 percent, or higher to achieve the desired goal.

Depending on when you're reading this, you most likely already have a good idea of how high rates needed to go to bring down inflation—I won't embarrass myself by venturing a guess. But, in theory, the right move by the Fed would be to raise rates a little at a time until that equilibrium is hit, and then perhaps a little bit more to push inflation down to a comfortable level.

However, controlling a $25 trillion economy isn't that simple. Raising rates slowly over time poses some risks—the biggest being stagflation.

Stagflation

Stagflation is an economic situation characterized by simultaneous inflation and recession. Inflation is typically a sign of a strong economy, but inflation alongside increasing unemployment and slowing economic growth can create a downward spiral. Stagflation can destroy the economy for years or decades. This is because all the tools the Fed has available to curb inflation will risk deepening the recession, and vice versa.

The U.S. last saw stagflation back in the 1970s, when regulation around wages and consumer prices, along with rising oil and energy prices, drove annual inflation to over 13 percent. At the same time, a weak economy and high unemployment meant low economic growth—and financial struggles for the average American.

From 1970 through 1982, the U.S. saw four recessions, with both inflation and unemployment consistently above 5 percent.

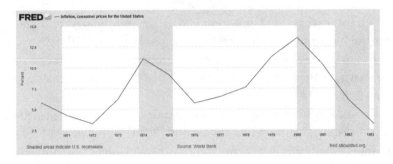

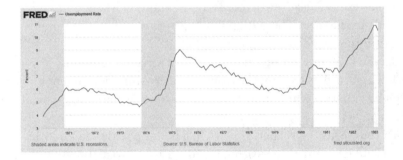

How do we avoid stagflation?

Again, we look to conventional wisdom, which says that to avoid stagflation, we need to raise rates quickly to shock the system, quash inflation, and get things back into the normal rhythm. While theoretically effective, raising rates slowly may be less effective—and riskier—than raising rates quickly and decisively.

Even if a quick spike in rates plunges the economy into recession, many people believe that it's better than risking a spiral into stagflation, which could cause a much worse and longer-lasting economic downturn.

As usual, though, it's not that simple. Raising rates quickly and drastically has an additional side effect that must be considered.

Risk of Debt Crisis

Raising rates too high too fast could cause an irreversible debt crisis.

When interest rates rise, bond yields (the interest paid to bond holders) also rise. Because treasury bonds are simply the debt that the U.S. has created, increasing interest rates means the government needs to pay more interest on the national debt. It's no different than taking a mortgage on a rental property: The higher the interest rate, the higher the interest payments, and the harder it is to cash flow.

When interest rates rise, bond yields rise, and the government must now spend more money on interest payments. This means the government either has to borrow more money (again at the higher interest rate) to pay all that interest, or the government needs to spend less money on everything it wants to pay for.

As we've seen over the previous four decades, the government is not very good at spending less money. In the case of quickly rising interest rates, the government would likely have to start issuing more debt to its interest payments, which would increase those interest payments, forcing even more debt to be created, leading to more money printing, which...

You get the idea. The national debt spins out of control, and we risk defaulting or restructuring all that debt.

As you can see, the Federal Reserve is in a major dilemma!

It was forced to act after the pandemic drove inflation, and now it is in a catch-22 situation where it risks stagflation or a debt crisis to alleviate that inflation.

Of course, as the reader, you are in a better position to know how this turned out (or is turning out), but it's likely a safe prediction that the Fed's actions will lead to some other circumstances that will require hard decisions and trade-offs to be made. It is these decisions, actions, and reactions that ultimately drive the economy up and down in repeating cycles.

Negative Interest Rates

Finally, I want to touch on a topic that isn't being talked about much these days, although it was a big topic of conversation back in 2018 when this book was originally written. Depending on the trajectory of interest rates over the next several years, it could be a hot-button issue again.

When the economy overheats, the Fed will hike rates to slow inflation, the economy will slow, and the Fed then drops rates to get the economy back on track. Historically, this cycle of raising and lowering interest rates lasts about two years. And, on average, the top-to-bottom decrease in interest rates to drive us out of recession is about 5 percent.

During the next recession, if interest rates are below 5 percent, there's a possibility that lowering rates back to 0 percent won't generate enough economic growth to get things back on track. If the Fed needed more firepower to spur economic growth, one option is to take interest rates into the negative. This is uncharted territory, so we don't know exactly how this would play out. But, we can theorize.

First, let's look at how negative interest rates work.

Remember, when you borrow money, you pay back the amount you borrow plus a little more. That "little more" is based on the interest rate—the lower the rate, the less the "little more" you need to pay back. When the interest rate is zero, that "little more" is zero. In other words, you pay back $1 for every $1 you borrow—no interest!

With negative interest rates, however, not only does the borrower not have to pay back the "little more," but the borrower actually repays *less* than they borrowed (ignoring fees and such). For example, if I borrow $100 at a negative interest rate, I may only have to repay the lender $98 instead of the full $100!

You might be asking, why would a lender loan money in a situation where they aren't even going to get the full amount back? The answer is that the lender may not have a better option. If they put that money in the bank, and the bank is paying negative interest, that means that the bank isn't going to return the full amount of the deposit. That's right—negative rates mean you're paying the bank to hold your money. A lender may be happier loaning money at negative 0.5 percent than putting that money in a bank account or bonds earning negative 0.75 percent. They lose less money that way.

So far, that doesn't sound too bad. Negative rates help us as investors, because not only do we borrow money cheaply but we also don't have to pay back the full amount!

In reality, it's not all good. In fact, negative rates have the potential to hurt all aspects of the economy, from individual investors to big companies, banks, and Wall Street. Let's look at some of the ways negative rates can have a huge negative impact on nearly everything.

First, successful investors tend to have a lot of cash, and they need someplace to put that cash. As real estate investors, if we want to take advantage of borrowing at negative interest rates, we need to put our cash somewhere other than the houses we're buying. Unfortunately, just like we're getting negative interest on the money we're borrowing, many investments are paying negative interest as well. It costs money to keep our cash in the bank; it costs money to put that cash in government or corporate bonds; it costs money to lend, etc.

While there will still be investments that pay returns above zero percent, those investments will be in such high demand that they will skew riskier than the return they provide. Overall, those other investments may not be worth the risk, and mathematically, it may be better just to put our money in the bank and pay them to hold it.

For poorer people, negative rates are even worse. They see their savings eroded away, and the small negative interest they are paying to the bank could be enough to drive them to insolvency. One big effect of very low or negative interest rates is that it drives the inequality gap, hurting poorer people more than it hurts wealthier people. Low rates have already exacerbated the wealth gap over the past decade—that would get much, much worse with negative rates.

Next, think about how negative rates would affect big companies in the United States. Berkshire Hathaway has more than $120 billion in cash, Apple has more than $200 billion, and Facebook has about $50 billion. How do you think their shareholders would feel about losing money on those cash reserves quarter over quarter? And when corporate balance sheets get ugly, our equities markets (i.e., the stock market) start to get ugly. Negative interest rates could have a massive impact on equity/stock prices.

Negative interest rates also run the risk of destroying bank profits. Sure, they get to pay back less than you deposit—but people are much less likely to deposit money at negative interest rates and much more likely to stash it under their mattress or in a hole in their backyard. Negative interest rates are typically very bad for banks, which causes issues that can trickle into the broader economy.

Lastly, negative interest rates in one country encourage citizens to ship their money to another country or another currency that might be paying a bit more (or that is less negative). This hurts the local currency and the local economy. It can also impact the country that's receiving that money, as it pushes down the returns for all investors in that market and hurts demand for domestic manufacturing, because imports are so much cheaper.

Again, much of this is just theory. Nobody knows exactly how negative interest rates would affect the economy long-term. That said, many economists speculate that things wouldn't end well.

This is one reason why a lot of economists suggest that the Fed raise rates as high as possible now, to avoid the risk of having to drop rates into negative territory during a future economic downturn.

CHAPTER 4

THE BUSINESS CYCLE

When we talk about economic cycles, what comes to mind for most Americans is the business cycle, which we talked about a good bit in Chapter Two. The business cycle is the cyclical expansion (strong economy) and contraction (weak economy) that we see about once a decade or so, and what we typically think of as basic economic fluctuations.

In this chapter I want to talk a little bit more about how the business cycle has manifested itself in the past, which will be important in later chapters when we're attempting to determine where we currently are in the cycle and how long we should expect to be there.

Remember, history tends to repeat itself, and economic cycles are no different. In fact, if anything, economic cycles tend to be more consistent than most things in history.

Important note:
Throughout the rest of this chapter and the rest of the book, I will be discussing the most typical impact that the business cycle has on the real estate market. That said, not every business cycle is built the same way, and not every cycle will have the same impact on real estate.

Some business cycle shifts will have a tremendously large impact on real estate in all geographic areas (like in the 2008 recession). Others will have a smaller impact (like in the 1990 recession). And others may impact certain geographic markets in to one degree while impacting other geographic markets to a much different degree (like in the 2001 recession). In fact, during some economic downturns, real estate is not impacted much at all, and may even strengthen in some markets (like in the 1980-1982 recession).

What we discuss here and throughout the rest of the book are the most common reactions the real estate market will have to a shifting economy but be aware that your market may react differently than others, and some economic cycles may not have the same real estate impact as others.

Length of the Business Cycle

According to the National Bureau of Economic Research (NBER), since 1854 there have been 34 business cycles in the United States. Prior to 1945, the average length of a business cycle was only about 51 months. Since 1945, the average length has grown to about 69 months.

Some have been shorter, while others much longer. In fact, the longest expansion (and that's just one part of the cycle) recorded by NBER lasted 128 months, from June 2009 to February 2020, when COVID-19 ended the long economic run after the Great Recession. While many people don't realize it, the eleven years between recessions from 2009 to 2020 was highly out of the ordinary and the longest in this country's history.

Here is a view of every cycle from 1860 through 2020, according to NBER.

PEAK MONTH	TROUGH MONTH	MONTHS PEAK TO TROUGH	MONTHS TROUGH TO PEAK	MONTHS PEAK TO PEAK
Oct 1860	Jun 1861	8	22	40
Apr 1865	Dec 1867	32	46	54
Jun 1869	Dec 1870	18	18	50
Oct 1873	Mar 1879	65	34	52
Mar 1882	May 1885	38	36	101
Mar 1887	Apr 1888	13	22	60
Jul 1890	May 1891	10	27	40
Jan 1893	Jun 1894	17	20	30
Dec 1895	Jun 1897	18	18	35

PEAK MONTH	TROUGH MONTH	MONTHS PEAK TO TROUGH	MONTHS TROUGH TO PEAK	MONTHS PEAK TO PEAK
June 1899	Dec 1900	18	24	42
Sept 1902	Aug 1904	23	21	39
May 1907	Jun 1908	13	33	56
Jan 1910	Jan 1912	24	19	32
Jan 1913	Dec 1914	23	12	36
Aug 1918	Mar 1919	7	44	67
Jan 1920	Jul 1921	18	10	17
May 1923	Jul 1924	14	22	40
Oct 1926	Nov 1927	13	27	41
Aug 1929	Mar 1933	43	21	34
May 1937	Jun 1938	13	50	93
Feb 1945	Oct 1945	8	80	93
Nov 1948	Oct 1949	11	37	45
Jul 1953	May 1954	10	45	56
Aug 1957	Apr 1958	8	39	49
Apr 1960	Feb 1961	10	24	32
Dec 1969	Nov 1970	11	106	116
Nov 1973	Mar 1975	16	36	47
Jan1980	Jul 1980	6	58	74
Jul 1981	Nov 1982	16	12	18
Jul 1990	Mar 1991	8	92	108
Mar 2001	Nov 2001	8	120	128
Dec 2007	Jun 2009	18	73	81
Feb 2020	Apr 2020	2	128	146

Source: **https://www.nber.org/cycles.html**

Note that while the lengths of a business cycle may vary, each has one very important factor in common: The expansions are almost always longer than the contractions.

Since 1945, the average expansion has lasted 58 months, while the average contraction lasted only 11 months. And, over time, it appears that this discrepancy between the length of the average contraction and the length of the average expansion is getting more pronounced:

	MONTHS PEAK TO TROUGH	MONTHS TROUGH TO PEAK	MONTHS PEAK TO PEAK
AVERAGES:			
1854-2009 (33 cycles)	17.5	38.7	56.4
1854-1919 (16 cycles)	21.6	26.6	48.9
1919-1945 (6 cycles)	18.2	35.0	53.0
1945-2009 (11 cycles)	11.1	58.4	68.5
1945-2009 (12 cycles)	10.3	64.2	75.0

While you'll notice that before I've been using a cute little symmetrical curve to represent the business cycle but, in actuality, the cycle looks more like this:

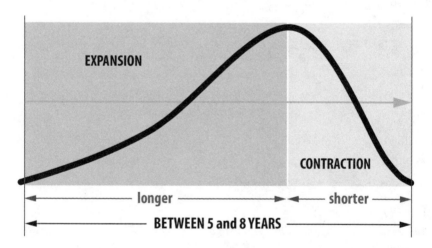

I don't mean to bog you down with data. In fact, there are only two important takeaways here that you need to keep in mind:

1. The average length of the business cycle is between five and eight years; and
2. The expansion part of the cycle is much smoother and longer—sometimes four or five times as long—as the contraction phase.

Because it's easier for me to draw and likely easier for you to remember, I'm going to continue to draw the cycle curve as the symmetrical curve I was using earlier in the book. But try to keep in mind that the actual cycle looks more like the image on the previous page.

Four Phases of the Business Cycle

So far, we've talked a lot about cycles in general, and we've dug a good bit into the business cycle and how it works. But this book is about investing, and how we should be modifying our investing strategies and tactics based on where we are in the economic cycle.

In order to accomplish this, we need to break the business cycle into pieces. This will allow us to focus our attention on each piece—each *phase*—of the cycle independently.

And then for each of those phases, we can identify things like:

- How do we know when we're in this phase?
- How do we modify our investing strategies and tactics for this phase?
- How do we prepare for the next phase in advance?

While it's completely arbitrary how many phases we break the cycle into, there are some good rules of thumb. Since we'll likely want to modify our strategies and tactics in each phase, breaking it into too many phases would require us to change strategies too often.

On the other hand, breaking things into too few phases would mean that we're not changing up our strategies often enough to accommodate the changing market.

When it comes to adjusting my real estate strategies, I've found that that four is the right number of phases. The four phases I've chosen are:

- The Expansion Phase
- The Peak Phase
- The Recession Phase
- The Recovery Phase

Here's how these four phases are represented on our business cycle curve:

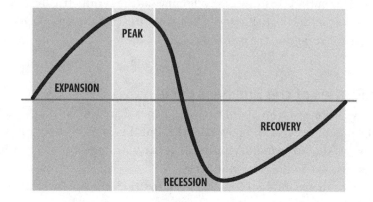

The cycle spends several years trending up through a period of economic expansion. It then plateaus at a peak, which generally lasts anywhere from a few months to a year. It declines during a period of recession and economic turmoil. And finally, as the recession comes to an end, the market starts to recover and again begins its upward trajectory.

As you can see, the phases aren't equal in length; like we discussed in the last section, the upswings (Expansion and Recovery phases) are typically much longer in aggregate than the downswing (Recession Phase).

Throughout the rest of the book I will be referring to where we are in the economic cycle based on these four designations. And we'll discuss each phase in much greater detail later.

But before we go any further, let's take a closer look at the characteristics that define each phase of the cycle from the perspective of a real estate investor.

Expansion Phase

In this phase of the cycle, buyer demand for housing increases as other economic factors such as wage and job growth are strong. Occupancy rates continue to increase as vacancies continue to decrease. Housing inventory is dropping, and new construction begins to meet the increasing demand.

Because demand is outpacing supply, prices increase—oftentimes faster than the rate of inflation. With confidence levels in both real estate and the broader economy high, those with money and those looking to make money turn to real estate.

Deals become scarce, and it's not unusual for investors to overpay for property during this phase of the cycle, thinking they'll be able to make their money back as prices and rents continue to rise. But as we know, what goes up must come down.

Peak Phase

At the peak of the cycle, prices hit a plateau and demand starts to soften. In some geographic locations, there aren't yet signs of a slowdown, but other locations are foreshadowing the economic changes with higher days on market for residential property and fewer new listings and buyers.

New construction continues to boom, as the units coming on the market during this phase have been in the works for months or years at this point. But the strong economy has been driving inflation, and around this time, the government steps in and raises interest rates to help combat that inflation.

Eventually the market reaches a point where the demand that was created during the Expansion phase has been met, and the available inventory exceeds the current demand. With excess inventory on the market, rising interest rates, and the first signs that the economy is starting to crack, we start to see real estate prices decline, and the downturn begins.

Recession Phase

During the Recession Phase, there's general economic turmoil. While every recession is different, some common elements include high unemployment, reduced wages, and tightening of credit.

For investors, this means an increase in the number of foreclosures, higher vacancies, fewer buyers, and reduced property values. As occupancy rates fall below the long-term average, we often see reduced market rents.

New construction quickly stops, and many partially finished projects go unfinished. It's not uncommon to see landlords drastically lower rents to attract new tenants and homeowners drop prices to attract buyers during this phase.

Recovery Phase

This is the phase of the real estate cycle when the previous decline starts to turn around. At the beginning of a recovery, real estate prices may continue to decrease, or they might plateau.

During this phase, it's common for the government to lower interest rates in an attempt to spur economic growth. Once the recovery gains momentum, inventory declines, and many distressed properties get scooped up by investors or savvy homebuyers. Buyer demand increases and prices may start to rise, but still tend to stay below the inflation rate.

New construction hasn't yet picked up, as financing is still tight and builders are likely still skittish. But builders start to come out of their slumber, begin to line up credit and financing, and look to build their portfolio of land for future development.

Why These Four Phases?

The decision to use four phases—and these specific four phases—to frame the discussion in this book was somewhat arbitrary.

It's not hard to justify only calling out two or three phases or instead calling out five or six phases. For example, I call out a "peak" phase where the market turns from good to bad, but I don't mention an analogous phase at the bottom where the market turns from bad to good.

Why did I choose the phases I did? There are a few reasons for this:

1. It's often difficult to distinguish exactly which phase we're in at the time we're in it. In many cases, it's only obvious that we've moved into another part of the cycle long after the transition has started. Having too many phases can easily add to this confusion. Four tends to be a good number. With the exception of the Peak Phase, each of these phases lasts several years.

2. You'll notice that the upswing is broken into two phases—expansion and recovery—while the downswing is a single phase—recession. The reason for this is that the upswing tends to be a good bit longer than the downswing, and the upswing tends to provide a variety of opportunities for real estate investors at different points. The downswing is typically more homogenous in terms of investing opportunity, and there isn't much difference between the beginning of that phase and the end of it.

3. I've included a phase at the top (peak) but not a phase as the bottom. That's because the peak of the cycle is a point of both great opportunity and risk, and a separate discussion of this part of the cycle is warranted. The transition at the bottom of the curve is much less interesting from the perspective of a real estate investor, so I don't need to address it specifically.

Inflection Points

In math, an *inflection point* is the point where a curve changes direction. In an economic cycle, the inflection points are the points at the very top and very bottom of the curve. They occur during the transition from the Expansion Phase to the Recession Phase (the phase that we call the peak) and the transition from Recession Phase to Recovery Phase.

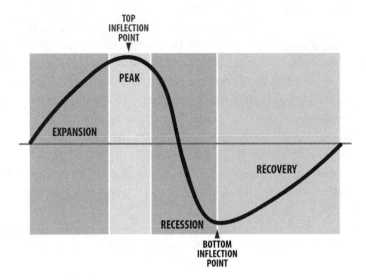

At the top inflection point, demand has dropped and supply has increased. They are briefly in balance—prices are not rising or falling—but soon supply will outpace demand and prices will start to fall. At the bottom inflection point, just the opposite happens. Supply falls, demand increases, and we hit a balance again. But this time, demand will outstrip supply and prices will start to rise.

In 2007-08, we saw a very quick and obvious inflection point where the market turned from strong to weak, and the recession came quickly. But inflection points aren't always quick reversals. The market may plateau for months or even years before it turns around.

From 2018 through 2020, before the pandemic, many experts believed that the market had peaked and plateaued. While we'll never know what would have happened had COVID-19 not hit, the data indicates a two-year peak in the market leading up to that point. And here in 2022, there's good reason to believe we may be at another market peak, though we don't yet know how long it will last or where it will head next.

You don't typically hear much about these two points in the cycle because they can be hard to identify in real time. In fact, we often don't realize we've reached an inflection point until we're well past it. But they're important because inflection points are the places where lots of money is either made or lost.

In 2007-08, millions of investors across all industries lost a substantial portion of their net worth—and many went bankrupt—because they weren't prepared for a quick turnaround in the economy. It's not uncommon these days to still hear horror stories from investors about how they lost millions of dollars in equity and assets over the course of just a few months.

On the other side of that coin, those investors who were prepared and well positioned for the bottom inflection point that we saw in 2010–11 made a killing. The recovery and expansion seen from 2010 through 2020 is considered to be one of the biggest transfers of wealth in the history of this country, and many investors have profited greatly from that turnaround.

Additionally, while it was much more short-lived and unpredictable, the run-up in housing values from 2020 through the beginning of 2022 was unprecedented. Many investors and average Americans alike were able to build a tremendous amount of equity during this brief period after the pandemic.

Long story short, understanding these inflection points and preparing yourself for them can mean the difference between great losses and great prosperity.

CHAPTER 5

KNOWING WHERE WE ARE IN THE CYCLE

As we've discussed, the real estate market aligns closely with the business cycle. When the economy is strong, real estate tends to do well; when the economy is weak, real estate tends to follow suit.

That's because many of the factors that impact the overall economy—wage growth, GDP (gross demostic product), unemployment—also impact the ability of consumers and developers to buy and sell real estate. When the economy is strong, interest rates are low, and incomes are rising. Individuals can afford to make large purchases such as buying a house, and developers are able to build and sell new construction.

But when the economy weakens, interest rates start to rise and wages stay flat. That's why you see increased vacancies at the end of the Peak Phase, during a recession, and at the beginning of a recovery. And it's why you see decreasing vacancies as the recovery gains momentum, during an expansion, and through much of the Peak Phase.

So how do we use this information to help us become better investors? The first step to harnessing the power of the economic cycle is to be able to determine what phase of the cycle we're in. That can be difficult to do, especially if we're just looking at real estate metrics. Too many people look at the housing market and use it to extrapolate the overall health of the economy. They see strong housing sales and rising prices and assume that the economic trajectory is a good one.

But that's not necessarily the case. Economic shifts can seemingly happen quickly, but to those who have been paying attention, the signs of an impending shift may have been around for a long time.

And because a good bit of real estate performance is localized, different geographic areas can appear to indicate that we're at different points in the economic cycle. This is especially true around the inflection points, where some parts of the country may seem to be reversing their current trend at the same time other parts of the country appear to be continuing that same trend.

Investors in Omaha, Nebraska, may think that real estate is on an upward path that will last for several years to come. At the same time, investors in Los Angeles, California, may be seeing a softening housing market, decreased home values, and longer days on market. Ask these two groups of investors where the economy is headed and they are likely to give you two very different answers.

To understand where we really are in the cycle, we have to dig deeper than just looking at where our local real estate market is today. Those who know how to track the economy can piece together clues to make an educated guess about where we *really* are in the current cycle.

For example, most experts would agree that at the time of this writing (again, mid-2022), the economy has peaked at a national level, and we are likely either in the Peak Phase or just past it, heading into the next downturn. Inflation has peaked, interest rates are on the way up, and all indications are that the Fed is planning to continue raising rates over the next few quarters.

What most economists don't agree on is whether we've hit the top inflection point already or not. Some say it already happened earlier in 2022 and we're now in the midst of the downturn. Unfortunately, it's difficult to know for certain until we're well past that point because economic data tends to lag by one to three months; we could currently be in a recession and not know it for a few more months.

So, if the experts can't always determine where we are in an economic cycle, how are the rest of us supposed to figure it out?

I like to use three major analysis tools when I'm considering where we may be in the cycle: observation, timing, and data.

Observation

While this is the least scientific of the ways you can assess where we are in the cycle, just looking at what's going on around you in terms of the economy and the real estate market can give you a reasonable indication of where things may be and where they may be headed.

For example, throughout most of the country, for the past several years we've seen a steady increase in real estate values across most asset classes such as real estate, the stock market, and corporate earnings. Based on this information, we can infer that we're currently in an upswing and are more likely approaching the top of the cycle, not the bottom.

Across many areas of the United States, observations of the real estate market, as well as observations of consumer confidence and behavior, indicate things are going very well—perhaps even too well. Many observers believe we're approaching the inflection point, while others claim we have already reached it. Because there's "irrational exuberance" in the market and many new investors coming out of the woodwork every day, there is reason to believe the real estate market is hotter than it's been for a long time.

Whether that means a downturn is right around the corner—or still months or years away—remains to be seen. But by observing what's going on at both local and national levels, it's safe to assume that we're closer to the top of the market than we've been in a long time. That means it's time to start considering how we'll change our strategy when signs of a downturn are more pronounced.

We'll talk a lot more about using observation to determine where we are in the cycle when we delve into each cycle later in the e-book.

Timing

Because business cycles tend to adhere to a rough schedule, we can use that information to determine where we might be in the current cycle.

If we look back to the first decade of this century, home values were rising. In fact, the average sale price of a new home in the United States increased by almost 40 percent from April 2003 ($237,000) to March 2007 ($329,000). Not only were we in an upswing, we were in the middle of the one of the hottest real estate and equity markets in history.

Now, if we were to look back at the market in 2009, we see a very different picture. The housing market had crashed, home prices in much of the country had dropped significantly, the stock market had tanked, and we were in a deep recession.

That was a decade ago. Given that the typical business cycle only lasts five to eight years, it wouldn't be unreasonable to assume that after ten years we should expect that we're overdue for another downturn, and that it may occur in the very near future.

In fact, as of this writing, we are currently in the midst of the longest economic cycle in modern history!

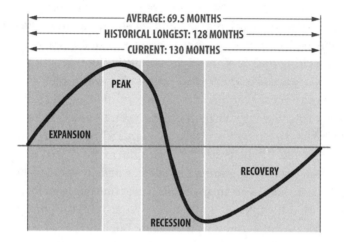

Unfortunately, this is also the problem with relying on timing. While it can be a good way to help you understand basic patterns, there's a big margin of error when it comes to actual prediction value. In other words, understanding the historical timing behind the business cycle can give us a general range for when we should expect things to change, but the actual timing for any one cycle can be off by several years.

If we had relied too much on timing during the cycle that started in 2008, we might have started changing up our investing strategies in 2014 in preparation for a recession. That would have been devasting to our businesses.

Data

While we've discussed using observation techniques and looking at the timing of past economic cycles to determine where we may be in the current cycle, the most reliable indicators of where we are and where we're headed are the data itself. That is how most economists interpret the current situation and direction of the market. If you want to be a successful investor in any industry, you should learn which economic data is important and how to interpret it.

When we know what to look for, economic data patterns can give us a lot of foresight into the market and where it's headed. Like the other two ways, economic data isn't going to be 100 percent accurate. It's not foolproof and it won't always tell the whole story. But when we understand what to look for in the data and we combine that information with what observation and timing is telling us, we can get a pretty good idea of where the market is going—and when.

There are literally thousands of factors that contribute to the performance of the general economy, as well as the real estate market in any given area. Some are more influential than others, and some provide greater predictive value about where the market currently is and where it's headed.

Before we jump into a discussion of the specific economic data we should be looking at, there's an important concept I want to discuss—leading versus trailing indicators.

Leading versus Trailing Indicators

There are two types of data indicators that can help us determine where we are in the current cycle as well as where we're headed. The first type is *leading indicators*. These factors shift before you see major changes in a specific market or the general economy. Think of them as precursors to change. They can help you predict what's going to happen next. When they shift, it's a sign that market and broader economic changes are coming.

For example, if a large company announces it's moving its headquarters to your city next year, that announcement is a leading indicator of subsequent changes that will occur in your area. Because leading indicators predict what lies ahead, you can adjust your strategy accordingly and take advantage of the opportunities—or hedge against the risks—those changes will bring. That's what my wife and I have been doing for the last decade. Because we've watched these indicators and have adapted our strategy when the market first begins to shift, we've been able to capitalize on opportunities other investors have missed.

On the flip side, *trailing indicators* are the results of shifts in a market or economy. Think of them as successors to change. Unlike leading indicators that warn you so you can adjust your strategy, trailing indicators show up after a change has already occurred. For example, after the large company moves its headquarters to your city, you'll likely see new jobs created, an influx of current employees relocating, increased traffic, and rising home values. These things—new jobs, increased home values—are trailing indicators of the company move.

Looking at leading indicators can help you make proactive decisions. If you were the first to know that a big company is relocating to a specific area, you could purchase property in that area and watch the value of your investment skyrocket once the announcement was more widely known. Trailing indicators—for example, the rise in home values after the company announcement—typically won't help you very much.

While it's often too late to make changes to your strategy after trailing indicators show up, that doesn't mean they have no value. On the contrary, they can help us learn. They show us what went well, what didn't, and what we need to change next time to be more successful.

Analyzing both leading and trailing indicators can help you recognize what phase of the economic cycle we're in and how quickly the next phase is approaching. If you use that information to your advantage, you can make changes to your investment strategy before the next cycle begins. But if you miss the indicators, or change too slowly, your business and your profits will likely suffer.

Also, keep in mind that to get a balanced perspective, it's important to look at both real estate and non-real estate indicators. Let's look at some of those now.

Non-Real Estate Indicators

There are many non-real estate indicators you can track to help you determine what phase of the economic cycle we're in and when the next phase might begin. Here are several I follow.

Yield Curve

The yield curve is an important economic concept that every investor should be familiar with. Simply stated, the yield curve represents the change in interest rates for government bonds of different expiration dates. Let me break that down...

Yield Curve #1

There are three things you need to understand here:
1. The government raises money by issuing and selling treasury bonds. Treasury bonds are simply an investment that pays a fixed amount of interest (also known as "yield") to the purchaser. Treasury bonds can be purchased by people like you and me, by corporations looking for a safe place to put their money, or even by countries looking to invest billions of dollars.

2. Treasury bonds have "expiration" periods. An expiration is an amount of time the purchaser needs to hold the bond before getting their principle investment back. You can buy short-term bonds (1 month, for example), long-term bonds (30 years, for example), and anything in between.

3. Typically speaking, shorter expiration bonds pay less interest (yield) than longer expiration bonds. This should make sense—if you're locked into a longer-term investment, you will generally want a better return, as you don't have access to that money should a better investment come along.

Given those three things, at any given time, we can plot a graph of different expiration bonds along with the amount of yield each one pays.

For example, this is what the yield curve looked like in January 2004, during a strong and vibrant economic expansion:

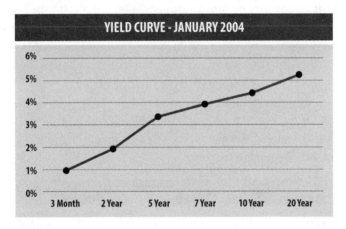

This plot of the yields for different expirations of treasury bonds is known as the "yield curve." And as you can see, this yield curve starts in the lower left and goes to the upper right.

A curve like this makes sense. For those people who are willing to invest their money for longer periods of time, the government provides higher returns.

Yield Curve #2

But the government doesn't set the amount of yield that these bonds pay. The returns are controlled by supply and demand.

When lots of people want to buy a particular expiration bond (high demand), the yield goes down. This makes sense—if a lot of people want in on an investment, the owner of the investment doesn't need to provide as much return to the investors. But, when there is little demand for a particular expiration bond, the yield goes up. Again, this makes sense—lower demand pushes yields up to encourage more investors to be willing to invest.

Why is this important?

Well, when investors start to get worried about the economy, the first thing they do is to move money out of short-term, risky investments and put that money into longer-term, more secure investments. And because long-term expiration treasury bonds are the most secure long-term investment on the planet, when investors get spooked about the economy, they will take money from their other investments—like real estate and the stock market—and put it in these long-term bonds.

Remember what we discussed above: When demand for a particular expiration bond goes up, the yield goes down. So, when investors start to get worried and move their money into long-term bonds, the yields begin to drop.

Likewise, when investors get worried, they don't want their money in short-term investments. So, during times of economic concern, investors will take money out of short-term expiration treasure bonds. This reduced demand on short-term bonds will drive their yields up.

As investors get more and more concerned about the economy, short-term bond yields increase and long-term bond yields drop—the curve *flattens*. This is what the yield curve looked like in March 2006, about 18 months before the Great Recession started:

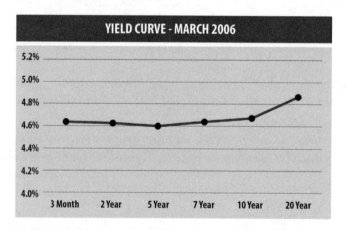

It turns out that the yield curve is one of the best predictors of an impending top inflection point in the economic curve. Right before a recession, we will typically see the yield curve go from flat to *inverted*, with the left and right ends of the curve higher than the middle.

This is what the yield curve looked like just a few months later in August 2006, about a year before the Great Recession started:

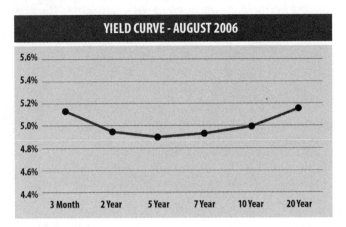

An inverted yield curve has been one of the most reliable predictors of a recession for the past century, and typically occurs between six and 18 months before the downturn is evident.

Unemployment

Unemployment statistics measure the percentage of people in the United States who are working versus out of work. There are several measures for this statistic, but the most common is referred to as the U3 unemployment rate. It's considered the *official* unemployment number and measures the percentage of U.S. residents who are out of work but have looked for work within the previous four weeks.

In a healthy economy, we expect the U3 unemployment rate to be in the range of 4 to 5 percent. When unemployment creeps above this mark, it's typically a signal that the economy is weakening. For example, in December 2007 (the beginning of the last recession), the national unemployment rate was 5 percent. But by the end of the recession in June 2009, it had increased to 9.5 percent. And in October 2009 it peaked at 10 percent—four months after the recession ended.

But, just like an increasing unemployment rate is cause for concern, so is a very low unemployment rate. When the unemployment rate gets down near 4 percent—and below—we generally consider the nation to be at *full employment*.

Full employment is good short term because it means many Americans are gainfully employed. However, it's also a precursor to inflation, which will be a drag on the economy. Full employment has historically been a signal that a downturn, or full-fledged recession, is right around the corner.

The following graph maps the unemployment rate over the past 70 years.[1] The gray vertical bars are recessions:

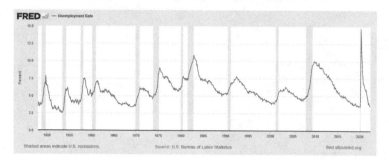

As you can see, full employment is almost always followed by a recession.

Stock Market

Stock prices reflect the predicted future strength of a company. Most companies perform well when the economy is strong and growing. So if the stock market is performing well it's likely the economy is too. But just like any market or economy, it can't continue an upward trajectory forever.

If the market has been steadily climbing for a long period of time, it's probably an indication that we're either nearing the end of an Expansion Phase or in the Peak Phase. Either way, we know a downturn will be coming at some point. On the flip side, if the stock market has been declining for an extended period of time, that's a sign we're in a recession. The length of the decline may help you identify how close we are to entering the Recovery Phase.

One interesting measure to track with respect to the stock market and the economic cycle is what's often called the "Buffett Indicator," named after famed investor Warren Buffett, who first mentioned this correlation in a 2001 interview. It's the idea that the value of all companies in the United States (which is reflected by the value of the overall stock market) should increase pretty much linearly over time.

Sometimes the stock market price will be above that imaginary increasing line and sometimes it will be below, but over time it will always trend back to that line. If we can determine where that line indicates the correct stock market price should be today, we can see if the market is higher than that (and likely to drop) or lower than that (and likely to rise).

The Buffett Indicator suggests that the total value of the stock market is directly related to the nation's GDP. We should be able to compare the value of the stock market to the GDP to determine whether the equities market (basically, the stock market) is correctly valued, undervalued, or overvalued.

The general consensus is that if the ratio of these two values is between 75 percent and 100 percent, the stock market is fairly valued. Under 75 percent means the market is undervalued. Over 100 percent means the market is overvalued.

The following chart maps the Buffett Indicator over the past 50 years.[2] The grey vertical bars are recessions:

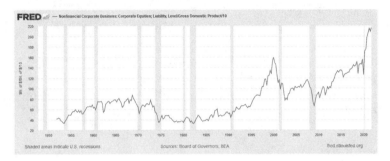

Notice that the Buffett Indicator has only been above 100 percent four times in the past 50 years, and all four times were followed by a recession within a couple years.

GDP

GDP is the total value of economic activity within a country and is an indicator of overall economic health. When GDP is increasing, the economy is growing. When GDP is decreasing, the economy is contracting.

Many experts agree the ideal growth rate for the GDP is 3 to 4 percent. Growth that exceeds this rate is often a sign of above average inflation, and the government may decide to increase interest rates to slow that inflation. As we've discussed, increasing interest rates will tend to put the brakes on a growing economy and can lead to reduced GDP or even negative GDP.

Growth that is below this 3 to 4 percent rate is often a sign of a weak economy. And in general, if GDP is negative for two or more quarters in a row, the economy is considered to be in a recession.

By tracking GDP, we can get a sense of where the economy is headed. Here is the chart mapping out the changing GDP rate over the past 70 years:[3]

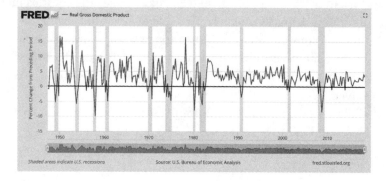

Notice that while not all dips below zero percent meant a recession was coming, you can again see by looking back at the last several recessions that there was a trend downward for the preceding year or so leading up to that recession.

Interest Rates

Low interest rates make it easier for consumers and investors to borrow money. Rates tend to be low during the recovery and expansion phases of the cycle as the government tries to fuel economic growth.

But, as we've discussed, when the economy grows too quickly, the government typically responds by raising interest rates to keep inflation in check. Unfortunately, that increase in interest rates means borrowing becomes more expensive and a larger percentage of income is being used to pay interest on credit cards, mortgages, and other types of loans.

The increased borrowing and interest costs to consumers and businesses can put a brake on economic growth. As rates rise, the economy slows, generally leading to a recessionary period.

Typically, interest rates will level off and then start to rise a year or two before a recession. Here is a chart of the federal funds rate—the rate at which the Fed loans money to banks—over the past 70 years:[4]

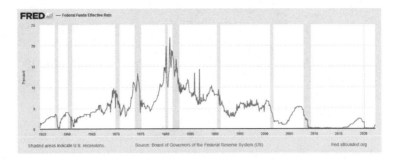

Notice the increase in rates shortly before each recession.

Wages

When the economy is strong and businesses are growing, businesses often pass some of their increased profits to their employees, increasing wages. But when the economy slows down, profits typically decrease, and wages either stagnate or decrease. Eventually, companies will start to lay off workers, unemployment increases, consumers can't pay their bills, and a downward economic spiral ensues.

Economists often look at wage growth as an indicator of whether employees and consumers will be either spending money—and driving the economy—or scrimping and saving because their paychecks are growing at a slower rate than inflation. When wage growth is lower than inflation, it's a sign that the overall economy is out of whack and economic challenges are looming.

Note that the current economic expansion, which started several years ago, has seen very anemic wage growth. After adjusting for inflation, most employees aren't earning any more these days than they were ten years ago. This is one of the reasons why a lot of economists believe the current economic expansion isn't as strong as many believe.

The following is a graph of hourly earnings—a good measure of wages—over the past 60 years:[5]

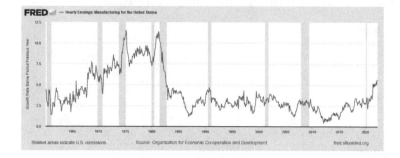

You'll notice that wages tend to drop about two to three years before a recession is declared.

Real-Estate Indicators

In addition to the non-real estate economic indicators I discussed above, there are also several real estate specific indicators I follow and also recommend that others follow:

Housing Supply

Although real estate markets are localized, and national trends may not represent what's happening in your area, there's value in looking at the national housing market. A good indicator of overall economic health is housing supply.

Housing supply is sometimes referred to as *housing inventory* or *days on market* (DOM), and is the average amount of time it takes to sell a house in a particular market. The more demand there is for housing, the less time a typical house stays on the market for sale before being put under contract.

On average, housing supply across the country is around six months. When supply drops below six months, there's more than average housing demand (the market is strong). When supply increases above six months, there's less than average housing demand (the market is weak).

Here is a chart of housing supply over the 60 years:[6]

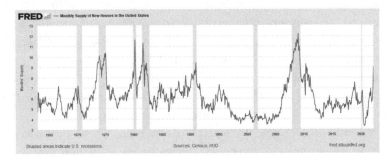

We'll talk about this a lot more in the next chapter, but notice that when housing supply starts to rise, a recession nearly always follows.

Housing Starts and Building Permits

The number of new residential units developers are starting to build is an excellent indicator of the amount of housing demand expected in a location. New construction will increase an economic expansion, when consumers have confidence in the market and plenty of disposable income. On the flip side, new construction usually decreases during the downturn as consumer confidence wanes and income growth stagnates.

The number of housing starts in an area—or the number of permits that have recently been issued—can provide valuable data about what phase of the real estate cycle your local market is in.

The following graph tracks housing starts over the past 60 years:[7]

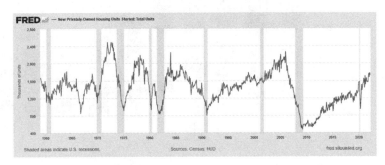

Notice that there tends to be a dramatic drop in housing starts immediately preceding each of the past eight recessions. Also notice that there have been some large decreases that didn't result in a recession (most notably in the mid-1960s), so this isn't a perfect indicator.

Foreclosures

Foreclosure rate is a powerful indicator of the strength of the real estate market and the economy in general. During an economic expansion, total foreclosures drop, as consumers have less trouble paying their mortgages and increased home values allow financially stressed homeowners to sell for a profit without defaulting on their mortgages.

But toward the peak of the cycle, as unemployment ticks up and inflation starts to impact how far paychecks will go, foreclosures start increasing. They continue to increase through the downturn, where they peak. The number and percentage of houses in foreclosure is a good indicator of where we are in the economic cycle.

The following chart tracks foreclosure filings from 2005 through 2017, and is indicative of what we expect to see during a run-up to a recession (2008) and then a recovery and economic expansion (2011 through 2017):[8]

Some Final Thoughts on the Economic Cycle

Remember, even if you're carefully following all the real estate and non-real estate economic indicators, it's not always clear where we are in an economic cycle or when the inflection points will occur. Sometimes, it's even difficult in hindsight!

This is especially true when the transition from one phase to another isn't immediate but takes place over time. Or when the economy stagnates at an inflection point or between two phases.

As you develop and refine your investment strategy for different phases, it's important to remember that all cycles are not equal. For example, the 2007-11 down market was much worse than normal. On the other hand, the 2001 market correction was shorter—and less impactful long term.

Every cycle—and every phase of every cycle—will have its unique conditions and circumstances. But if you're prepared for the phase changes, and if you understand the basic concepts around investing during each of the phases, you and your business can thrive, regardless of what the economy throws at you.

One final word before we move to Chapter Six and examine investing factors in detail. Because the real estate market is local, your area or a certain asset class in your area may be in a different phase of the cycle than other parts of the country. Or you might be in the same phase but experiencing it to a different degree than other areas.

For example, during the downturn a decade ago, virtually every market in the country experienced a drop in real estate prices, but some markets got hit much harder than others. That's why it's important to not only pay attention to what's happening on a national level but also in your own backyard.

CHAPTER 6

INVESTING FACTORS

If you've never been through a full economic cycle, it's natural to assume the major difference between an up real estate market and a down real estate market is simply the value of properties. After all, when the market's strong, so are property values; and when the market weakens, property values decline.

While the value of property is certainly one of the real estate market factors impacted by fluctuations in the economy, it's far from the only one. In this chapter, I'm going to discuss some of the other impacts a fluctuating economy has on real estate investing and how these factors contribute to how easy or difficult it is for real estate investors to earn—and keep—a profit.

Before I jump into what influences real estate investing throughout a market cycle, I want to discuss why the real estate market (and really any market) goes through major changes as the broader economy goes up and down.

Equilibrium and Supply and Demand

You've probably heard the word *equilibrium* before. By itself, it means balance. Two things are in equilibrium when neither side is exerting more force than the other.

In economics, the term equilibrium is often used to describe the state where supply (the amount of product available) and demand (the number of a products people want to buy) is about equal. In other words, when the number of people willing to purchase a product at a specific price is equal to the number of products sellers have available at that price, then that market is in equilibrium.

In the retail world, when supply and demand are in equilibrium, it means stores have no problem keeping the product in stock, but they don't also need to offer discounts to get consumers to buy them.

When supply and demand are *not* in equilibrium, either the consumer or the seller suffers. For example, when stores don't have enough inventory (supply) to satisfy all the customers (demand), the customers suffer. Customers may spend time waiting in lines, fighting over products, or even resorting to paying more than the retail price to get their hands on an item. Perhaps one of the best examples of this phenomenon is in the long lines you see on Black Friday as customers clamor to get the hottest toys or electronics for Christmas. These products are almost certain to sell out within hours and may not be back in stock in time for the holiday.

This often creates chaos, as consumers jockey for position in line, hoping to be one of the lucky few who will walk away with what they came for. If they don't, they might turn to a site like eBay, where those same products are being sold for more than retail price, as sellers know consumers are willing to pay more than what the product is worth.

On the other hand, there are times when stores can't sell things they've had in stock for months. These items take up valuable shelf space that could be used for other products that would sell more quickly. In these circumstances, it's not an unusual for stores to put the items on sale and, in some cases, they may be even pull the products from their shelves and give up trying to sell them at all.

We frequently see this after major holidays. Prices on the Fourth of July, Halloween, and Valentine's Day decor, crafts, and clothing get slashed as soon as the holiday is over, as most people are no longer interested in buying them. This is when the seller typically loses money on the remaining inventory.

Supply and demand are rarely in perfect equilibrium. That means that most of the time either the buyer or the seller has an advantage. When the economy is strong, and consumers are earning more, they spend more, so demand outpaces supply. The seller is at an advantage, so companies raise prices and produce more to meet the increased demand. Sellers continue to sell more at higher prices as long as the economy remains strong.

But when companies reach a point where either they've produced too much and the supply is greater than demand, or consumers can no longer afford to buy the products, there's a surplus. To get rid of the surplus, sellers begin reducing prices, giving the buyer an advantage.

This back and forth between supply and demand is always at work, creating the ups and downs we experience in various markets throughout the cycle.

Buyer's Markets and Seller's Markets

The real estate market works the same way I previously described. Real estate agents often refer to housing *supply*, which, given the current *demand*, is the number of months it would take to sell all of the houses currently for sale.

As an example, if a particular town sells an average of 20 houses per month and that town has 100 houses for sale, we'd say the town has about five months of housing inventory available. That's how long it will take, given the average number of houses being sold each month (20), to sell all 100 houses listed for sale.

But the housing market isn't static. The amount of inventory available can change quickly based on market conditions. There are two main factors that impact the housing supply currently available:

1. **The average amount of time it takes to sell a house.** In our example above, if the town were only selling ten houses per month, it would take ten months to sell the same 100 houses listed for sale.

2. **The number of houses listed for sale.** In the same example, if the town were selling 20 houses per month, but had 200 houses listed for sale, it would also take ten months to sell the inventory.

In both situations, the housing supply doubled—from five months to ten months—based on changes to the time it takes to sell a house (demand) and the number of houses for sale (supply).

In the real estate market, these conditions—supply and demand—are interrelated. That is, it's unlikely for the time it takes to sell a house to increase without the number of houses for sale also increasing. For example, if someone is thinking about selling their house and realizes the average time it takes to sell a house in their area is increasing, they're more likely to list it sooner because they know it will probably take longer to sell.

This increases housing supply. When supply increases, it typically takes longer to sell it all. And so it continues, creating a cycle that feeds on itself, leading a market that was once in equilibrium to quickly become out of balance.

We touched on this in the last chapter, but if you look at historical data of the national housing market, you'll see that in many areas of the United States, the average amount of housing supply is about six months.[9]

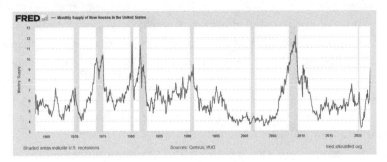

In other words, about six months is what's considered equilibrium in many real estate markets across the country. When there's less than a six-month supply on the market, it usually means sellers are in control because demand exceeds supply. More people want to buy houses than want to sell them, so buyers are competing for the same properties, which drives up prices. This is known as a *seller's market*.

On the other hand, when there's more than a six-month supply of houses on the market, it usually means buyers are in control. There are more houses for sale than people to buy them. The lack of interested buyers means sellers need to compete against one another to sell their properties. Often, sellers will lower their prices to attract buyers. This is known as a *buyer's market*.

This notion of supply and demand is what drives the strength of the real estate markets. Because the broader economy tends to dictate whether buyers have the means to make home purchases, it also tends to dictate whether we're in a buyer's or seller's market.

When the broader economy is strong, buyers have more ability to purchase housing, demand increases, and sellers have an advantage. In other words, when the economy is strong, we typically have a seller's market.

When the broader economy is weak, average buyers have less ability to purchase housing, demand decreases, and the few remaining qualified buyers have an advantage. In other words, when the economy is strong, we typically have a buyer's market, even if there are numerically fewer buyers who can take advantage of it.

Impact of the Cycle on Investing Factors

Now that you have a better understanding of what drives real estate prices up and down, I want to talk about how the broader economy impacts various factors that push the real estate market out of equilibrium, giving control to either buyers or sellers.

This is important because it will inform our judgment about which real estate strategies are most likely to work in the various phases of the cycle and which strategies are likely not to work—or worse yet, get us in trouble. In addition, understanding how the cycle impacts key investing factors will help us hone the specifics tactics we'll use to optimize our profits and reduce our risk.

Interest Rates

Interest rates are a major factor influencing whether an investor earns a profit and how much of one they earn. Interest rates dictate the cost of borrowing money, and they're important to real estate investors for two reasons:

1. When interest rates are high, investors must pay more to borrow money for their investments, which means the total cost of those investments is higher. When interest rates are low, investors pay less to borrow money, which means their total cost is lower. When investment costs are low, profit potential increases, but when investment costs are high, profit potential decreases.

2. Typical families who want to buy a home won't be able to pay as much for a property when interest rates are high as they can when interest rates are low. That's because interest rates impact their monthly mortgage payments just like they impact an investor's monthly loan payments. For example, if someone can borrow $400,000 when interest rates are 3.5 percent, if they want to keep their monthly payment the same when interest rates rise to 5.5 percent, they will only be able to borrow about $315,000.

3. For real estate investors who rely on selling properties, high interest rates can be troublesome. When rates go up, investors get squeezed from both ends. First, they have to pay more for their investments. Then, because buyers can't afford to borrow as much when interest rates increase, they typically sell their properties for less than they would if rates were low.

4. Lenders will see interest rates differently. When interest rates are high and other lending is tight, lenders have a great opportunity. Of course, that opportunity comes with greater risk, so lenders must

also modify their tactics throughout the cycle as rates change and the investing landscape shifts.

5. As we've discussed previously, expect interest rates to be lowest throughout the Expansion Phase. As we get into the Peak Phase, inflation will increase, leading the Fed to increase interest rates to discourage spending and slow the economy. Rates will likely increase into the recession, and then, to spur growth, will start to drop just before the bottom of the cycle. During the Recovery Phase, the drop in rates will slow and eventually level off.

Cap Rates

While margins are a good measure of return on a property that you're buying and selling, the capitalization rate (or just "cap rate") is one preferred measure of financial return used to evaluate an income producing property, such as an apartment complex. In simple terms, the cap rate is the income generated by the property divided by the value of the property.

For example, if a property is bought for $1 millionand has an annual income of $100,000 for the owner, the cap rate is 10 percent.

Cap rates tend to be consistent across similar properties in a geographic area. If a 100-unit Class B apartment complex in the Western Hills of Cincinnati, Ohio, has a cap rate of 8 percent, another apartment complex of similar size and condition in the same vicinity should be expected to have about the same cap rate. This makes sense—if an investor could get a much better deal on a similar property in the same area, why would they buy the worse deal?

Cap rates tend to move in cycles. As the economy improves, investors become desperate to find deals where they can invest their capital. As their desperation increases, they start paying more for cash-flowing assets, even if those assets aren't generating more income than they previously were. Higher prices for assets that are generating the same amount of income pushes cap rates down.

For example, the property above that sold for $1 million and was generating $100,000 per year in income may now sell for $2 million and still generate that same $100,000 per year. The cap rate has dropped from 10 percent to 5 percent.

When cap rates drop too low—because the price to buy is too high compared with the income-generating potential of the property—investors decide that the effort and risk associated with the investment isn't worth it, and they move to other investments with higher returns. Why invest in a risky and high-effort investment like an apartment complex for a 4 percent return when you can put your money into a long-term certificate of deposit and get a risk-free 3 percent return with no effort?

This reduction in demand forces owners to sell for lower prices, which means cap rates start to increase. That $2 million building may now be selling for closer to the $1 million it sold for a few years previously. Meanwhile, the income it generates hasn't changed. As cap rates start to rise, investors again flock to those deals, driving up demand, and again driving down cap rates.

This continual back and forth between sellers and buyers tends to keep cap rates cycling within a relatively narrow band throughout the market cycle. However, there are external forces that can push cap rates up or down, sometimes even outside of that typical band.

These factors include:

- **Interest rates.** When interest rates increase, investors can get better returns on risk-free investments like treasuries, bonds, and certificates of deposit, which decrease demand for low-return investments and drive cap rates up. When interest rates drop, the opposite happens. Investors get lower returns on risk-free investments, which increase demand for low-return investments and drive cap rates down. In the exceptionally low interest rate environment we've seen during the past few years, investors are buying properties that are generating less return than a typical savings account was generating in the last decade.

- **Vacancy rates.** When vacancy is high, properties typically generate less income, which reduces their value and decreases demand. When demand decreases, sellers lower their prices to attract more buyers, which increases cap rates. During periods of extremely high vacancy—like the depths of a recession or when there is considerable overbuilding in the area—cap rates can rise above the high end of the band. On the other hand, when vacancy rates are low, properties generate more income, increasing their value, and cap rates drop.

- **Availability of money.** When it's easy to borrow money, there's a lot of competition for properties, which drives prices up and cap rates down. At the same time, when money is plentiful, investors can borrow at lower rates, so they can accept lower returns on their investments, which also contributes to lower cap rates. On the flip side, when money is tight, it's more difficult for investors to borrow, so there's less competition for properties. And when interest rates are higher, borrowers are unable to accept low returns on their investments. If an investor is paying 8 percent in interest on their loan, it's unlikely they'll be willing to accept an investment that's only generating a 4-percent return.

If you're interested in *buying* investments that generate cash flow, buying during times of higher cap rates will position you to make more profit, both from increased cash flow and from an increase in property values when cap rates drop. These higher cap rate environments typically occur during the recession and recovery phases.

On the other hand, if you're ready to *sell* your income-generating property, you'll want to do so when cap rates are low because that's when sale prices are the highest. It's often best to do this during the expansion and peak phases when there's a lot of competition among buyers, money is cheap and readily available, vacancies are low, and properties are generating maximum income.

All that said, there are many historical situations where commercial real estate and cap rates haven't aligned with the business cycle. If interest rates and cap rates present a good opportunity to buy—or sell—during times when you otherwise wouldn't expect it, don't hesitate to jump on the opportunity

Profit Margins

For our purposes, we're going to think of profit margins—or just "margins"—as the most general ROI calculation (even though that's not entirely accurate from an accounting standpoint). Margins are simply the percentage amount that a business's profits exceed its expenses. It's most applicable to investor strategies that involve buying and reselling quickly—flipping, wholesaling, development, and quick land flips.

Much of the profit margin that's made by flipping or wholesaling is generated by buying below market value and selling at or above market value. When property values are rising, it's possible to expand your margins by simply waiting, as the value of the property will increase between the time you buy and the time you sell. For this reason, we often see margins increase during phases of the cycle when property values are increasing, which includes the recovery and expansion phases, and early in the Peak Phase.

On the flip side, the opposite happens when the value of your assets is decreasing. If the value of your flip property decreases between the time you buy and the time you sell, your margins will be smaller than if values were not dropping. In some cases, the decline in value can wipe out your profits altogether.

This isn't just the case for those buying and selling property. For lenders, when their interest rates are significantly higher than bank rates—for example, during the recession and recovery phases—margins are higher than when they have to loan at rates that are more in line with bank rates. For landlords, profit margins will increase when rents increase, when occupancy increases, and when turnover is low. For note buyers, margins tend to increase when borrowers are defaulting on loans and notes can be purchased for pennies on the dollar.

If you're in a situation where the value of whatever asset you're purchasing is decreasing—or could start decreasing before you plan to sell—your expected margins need to be big enough to overcome any potential drop in value that may occur, so you can still earn a profit.

For example, if you expect a 20 percent profit margin on a particular investment, you can only afford for prices to drop by 20 percent before you start to lose money on it. That should be obvious, but you'd be surprised at how many investors don't think in these terms.

By the way, this concept is especially important for deals that take a long time (big flips and development deals, for example), as markets can change considerably over several months or years, before the deal is complete.

Risk

This part of the discussion is directed toward the lenders out there—not just the professional or hard-money lenders, but also toward anyone lending from their personal funds (private lenders) or investing in syndication deals (passive investors).

It's important to evaluate the risk before implementing any investment strategy, but it's especially important when it comes to lending. While there are several factors that impact loan rates, including the rate set by the Fed and borrower demand, the amount of risk a lender assumes will be one of the biggest factors used to determine loan interest rates. Borrowers who lenders consider to be high risk will pay higher interest rates than those who lenders consider to be low risk. Risk is determined by the likelihood the loan will be repaid on time.

In general, lenders adjust rates based on two types of risk: market risk and deal risk.

Market Risk

Market risk is the risk associated with a deal based on current market conditions. For example, the risk on loans for flipping tends to be low throughout the Expansion Phase and into the Peak Phase. The likelihood flippers won't be able to resell a property during these phases is low, and even if they can't resell, values are rising, so it's unlikely borrowers will default on their loans during this phase, decreasing the risk to lender.

But as the market approaches the top inflection point, the risk to lenders who lend to flippers increases dramatically. If prices start to drop before investors can sell their properties, not only are investors more likely to default, but if they do, lenders will have to take back a property that's not worth as much as it was when they made the loan.

I often see lenders charging their lowest rates just before a market down-turn because they believe this is what they need to do to compete with other lenders during this period. However, as a lender, it's worth asking yourself whether it's better to sit on the sidelines for a few months during this phase than lend at rates that are too low to account for the risk during this period.

On the other side of the coin, I've often seen lenders jacking up rates con-siderably near the end of the Recession Phase and into the Recovery Phase. While this is an excellent time to generate large profits with these high rates, many lenders lose customers to small banks willing to lend at significantly lower rates. In my opinion, this is an excellent time for lenders to reduce their rates (risk is low at this point in the cycle), increase their volume, and build strong customer relationships that will carry into the next phases of the cycle.

Long story short, market risk is the risk associated with all aspects of the transaction outside of the specific borrower or deal.

Deal Risk

Deal risk is determined by the creditworthiness of the borrower and the risks associated with the specific deal they want to finance. Any loan can be either low or high risk at any point in the cycle, depending on the specifics of the deal.

For example, a deal would be low risk if a lender is:

- Lending a small portion of the total value of the property or asset.
- Lending to a very experienced investor.
- Lending to an investor with significant assets who's willing to sign a personal guaranty on the loan.

When the deal risk is low, the lender can accept a lower return and still have the same *expected value* (the statistically determined most likely amount) of profit across the total number of loans in their portfolio.

On the other hand, a deal might be considered high risk if the lender is:
- Lending close to the full value of the property.
- Lending to a new or inexperienced investor.
- Lending to a borrower with few assets that can be used for collateral on the loan.

On high-risk deals, lenders need to earn a higher return to get the same expected value across their portfolio.

In my experience, too many lenders set their interest rates without considering the details of the specific deal or the experience of the investor. That's a mistake, as evaluating each borrower and deal individually can provide the insight needed to undercut competitors when demand is high and risk is low. It can also reduce risk when demand is low and risk is high.

Appreciation

Appreciation is the increase in a property's value over time. I'm not a big fan of investing for appreciation over long periods of time because historically, in many areas of the country, real estate values don't tend to increase much more than the rate of inflation. Unless you're investing in an area where appreciation tends to outpace inflation, you may find that your profits don't live up to your expectations or long-term goals.

However, there is a time when this axiom doesn't hold true, and that's when there's a housing bubble. During the run up, home prices tend to increase much faster than the rate of inflation, as we saw from 2004 to 2007 and 2014 to 2018. But when the crash comes, home values drop, and even during the Recovery Phase, values often don't reach the rate of inflation. In a worst-case scenario, it can take several years for home values to return to pre-crash levels. Depending on other external factors, some markets may never fully recover.

While I don't recommend investing to capitalize on gains from long-term appreciation, it may make sense to capitalize on gains from appreciation that occurs from one phase of the real estate cycle to the next. For example, if you buy during the phases when values are dropping and sell during the phases when values are rising, you can make a good profit. This is especially lucrative for investors involved in land banking, long-term flip deals, and development.

This also provides an opportunity for those investors who do "live-in flips"—investment deals where the buyer lives in the property for at least two years to minimize their tax burden on any profits generated. We'll discuss this in more detail later, when I provide strategies and tactics.

Labor and Material Prices

We've discussed that when the economy improves, wages tend to increase. The real estate market is no exception. When the economy is strong, labor prices increase because contractors have lots of potential customers, and they can be choosy about who they do business with. On the other hand, when the economy declines—and construction slows—contractors are often willing to work for less.

We see the same trend with materials prices. When the economy is strong and construction volume increases, the demand for materials increases, which drives up prices. But when there's a downturn in the economy, there's less construction volume and less demand for materials, and prices will drop.

If you employ strategies that rely on the expense of contractors and materials, you'll find that during certain parts of the economic cycle—the expansion and peak phases, specifically—you're spending a lot more time, effort, and money to source good contractors and reasonably priced materials.

Size and Price of Properties

Larger properties tend to be more expensive than smaller ones. But these properties become more affordable to consumers when they're earning more and interest rates are low, which typically happens when the economy is strong. That's why we tend to see the average property size desired by buyers increase as the market improves.

On the other hand, the average property size buyers look for typically decreases when the market weakens, because consumers are earning less and interest rates are higher, meaning they can't afford to spend as much on a home.

The first segment of the real estate market that's affected when we're near the top inflection point consists of the larger and more expensive houses. In many cases, properties at the top of the price range will start seeing increased days on market and reduced sales well before smaller and less expensive properties.

For house flippers, this is especially important to note. When flipping toward the top of the market, houses at the top of the size and price range are the most likely to be difficult to resell. Additionally, higher priced properties are less likely to cash flow, so house flippers rarely have the ability to convert a failed high-end flip to a long-term rental property.

Ease of Finding and Selling Deals

As the real estate market moves up and down, the ease with which you can buy and sell properties fluctuates too. In a buyer's market, it's easy to find deals, but harder to sell them. In a seller's market, it's easy to sell properties, but harder to acquire them. As the cycle fluctuates, the balance changes and moves back and forth between being easy to buy and being easy to sell.

So why does this matter to you as an investor? Because some investment strategies rely on you being good at buying, while some rely on you being good at selling. If you're good at both, you can be successful at any point in the cycle. But if you're only good at one, you'll struggle at the points in the cycle where it's either more difficult to sell or more difficult to buy. There are few strategies that work well during all phases of the cycle, and those that do tend to work better in some parts of the cycle than other parts.

You'll typically see that it's easy to find and buy good deals during the recession and recovery phases because there's less competition from other investors, and sellers are desperate to get rid of property over concerns that values could continue to drop. But that makes it hard to sell during these times. So it's generally a good idea to focus on *buy-and-hold* strategies during these phases.

On the other hand, you'll generally see that it's tough to find great deals during the Expansion Phase because competition from other investors increases, and sellers know their property values are rising. The good news is that in a strong economy, lower interest rates and less stringent lending restrictions make it easy to sell during this phase. As a buyer, you may not be able to find the deal of a lifetime, but because it's easier to sell, you can still make a decent profit.

In some cases, it's hard to both buy and sell, and this is where investors run into problems. This is most common right around the inflection points. They're the trickiest parts of the cycle, and later in the book we'll talk about strategies that can help you keep moving forward and making money during these times.

The changes in the market that make it easy to sell during one phase and difficult to sell during another are why it's important to have a well-rounded investment strategy in place that allows you to be flexible, so you can take advantage of the opportunities the market presents and remain profitable no matter what phase of the cycle you're in.

Of course, not all real estate strategies fit this mold. Some strategies are more *countercyclical*, meaning they work better during the parts of the cycle where other strategies aren't working well.

For example, profitable notes can be found throughout all phases of the cycle. Lending can be more profitable when the economy is in turmoil.

The ease with which you can find and sell deals throughout the cycle is going to be highly dependent on the types of deals you're interested in buying and selling. This is even more reason why it's important to understand the cycle—so you can modify your strategies and tactics to focus on those that are best positioned to make you money.

CHAPTER 7

THE FINANCING FACTOR

In the last chapter, we discussed many of the factors impacting real estate investors as the economy shifts and we move into and out of specific phases of the cycle. I saved the most important factor for last—and decided to devote an entire chapter to it.

That factor is financing. Not only is it the most important part of most investing businesses, it's also going to be impacted more than nearly any other component of your investing business as we move through the various economic phases.

This is because financing affects two sides of our business.
First, it will impact our ability to acquire investments. Few of us have the luxury of purchasing our real estate investments using only cash we have available. Most of us require outside financing when we purchase our properties, and if our ability to borrow is reduced, so is our ability to acquire our inventory.

Second, for many of us, our customers are impacted by what's going on in the lending world. For any investors who sell property—flippers, wholesalers, value-add multifamily investors, and some land sellers—our customers will often need to borrow money to purchase our inventory. If our customers don't have the ability to borrow, or if their ability to borrow is reduced, we can't make our profit on the back end of our strategy.

For these reasons, it's important for us to understand how lending and financing are impacted throughout the cycle. We can then translate this information into strategies and tactics that allow us to continue to earn profits and reduce risk, even when lending is negatively affected.

Let's start with an overview of the types of lending that are most used in the real estate investing world, and who is most dependent on each. The following chart shows the most common types of real estate financing and which parties are most affected when that type of lending changes.

Below that, we will discuss the specific impact that each type of lending will have on investors—and our customers—throughout the various phases of the cycle.

TYPE OF LENDING/ LENDER	WHO IS IMPACTED?
Conventional lenders	Homeowners House flippers Landlords Multi-family investors Commercial investors
Portfolio lenders	House flippers Wholesalers Landlords Multi-family investors Hard money lenders
Hard money lenders	House flippers Landlords
Private lenders	House flippers Non-traditional investors Hard money lenders
Passive investors	Multi-family investors Commercial investors
Crowdfunding	House flippers Multi-family investors

Conventional Lenders

A conventional lender is typically a big bank or mortgage broker that facilitates loans insured by government agencies or quasi government agencies like Fannie Mae, Freddie Mac, FHA, or VA—all the big organizations you've probably heard about that make loans to consumers. These types of loans are generally used by homeowners who are buying houses that they are flipping or selling. Remember, as investors, we run a business, and we rely on our customers to be able to buy what we sell.

If conventional loans are not available to our customers, they can't buy our products. So the availability of conventional loans will have a direct correlation on whether our businesses are able to succeed using certain investing strategies. When it's difficult to get conventional loans, it's difficult for many of us, including house flippers and wholesalers, to survive. When it's easy for our customers to get conventional loans, house flippers and wholesalers will thrive.

But it's not just our customers who rely on conventional loans. Many mom-and-pop landlords rely on conventional lending for the success of their business. Conventional lenders are some of the few who will provide buy-and-hold investors full 30-year amortized loans at low interest rates. For that reason, the ease of getting conventional loans will have a big impact on whether small landlords can generate the cash flow they desire.

Next, the availability of conventional financing is going to have a big impact on large multifamily investors. It's these investors who often rely on conventional loans to purchase their multimillion-dollar complexes. And many of these investors do syndications or group money raises, and rely on conventional lenders for large down payments or to refinance as part of their exit strategy. This means that *their* investors rely on these conventional loans as well. When it's difficult to get or refinance conventional loans, both apartment syndicators and their investors will suffer.

Finally, commercial investors often rely on conventional financing. Investors who purchase assets like mobile home parks, self-storage facilities, office space, warehouses, and retail space often have few alternatives to conventional financing.

Long story short, the availability of conventional financing has perhaps the biggest impact on real estate investors of any other factor.

How does conventional lending get impacted throughout the cycle?

During the expansion part of the cycle, interest rates are low, the economy is strong, and the government will loosen up conventional lending requirements. This means that homeowners will be able to get cheap loans for their houses. It's not uncommon to see 10 percent down loans, 5 percent down loans, and even 3 percent down loans. And homeowners typically don't need fantastic credit scores to get loans—many loan programs will lend to people who have a credit score as low as 620. It's not very common that a flipper will run into buyers who can't get approved for a home loan, so selling their flips is easy.

Also, because interest rates are low and money is flowing easily through the banks, this means that landlords, multifamily investors, and commercial investors are also able to get easy financing to build up their portfolio of properties.

As we get toward the peak of the cycle, interest rates are rising, but the availability of conventional loans to homeowners isn't changing much. Loans still have low down payments, require just marginal credit scores, and are easy to get through underwriting. In other words, while homeowners may be able to afford a little bit less due to higher interest rates, it's still easy to get loans. Investors looking for commercial or multifamily loans may start to see things tighten up a little as interest rates rise, but again, money is still flowing easily through the banks, even to investors.

As we get over the peak and toward the Recession Phase, credit becomes tighter. The government will slow down on lending to homeowners, down payments will jump from 3 percent and 5 percent up to 20 percent, and suddenly, banks will be looking for homeowners to have credit scores of 680 or even 720! Keep in mind that typical Americans are starting to suffer financially at this point, and for many, credit scores are going down, not up. These increased credit requirements from banks will have a doubly negative effect on getting home loans.

For flippers especially, this is devasting to the business. Even if we can find good deals, selling them is very tough during a recession. For landlords and commercial investors, things aren't much better. Banks like working with investors when the economy is doing well, but will start to shun investors when the economy is on the decline. Loans are still available for investors with strong income, credit, and assets; but without all three, conventional loans are pretty much off the table.

As we get toward the bottom and the economy starts to recover, conventional lending tends to improve more slowly than the economy or the housing market. Banks are still shoring up their balance sheets, still licking their wounds from the previous recession, and are slow to start opening up the money spigot again.

Then as we near the end of the Recovery Phase and enter the expansion, we get back to low down payments, lower credit requirements, and money flowing easily once again.

Portfolio Lenders

Portfolio lenders tend to be small banks that loan their own funds—the money of their depositors—instead of loaning government secured funds. This means that the banks have the ability to define their own lending criteria and aren't hamstrung by the requirements of large government organizations. For this reason, small banks are often a great way for real estate investors to fund both non-traditional investments, like flips, as well as more traditional investments like buy-and-hold real estate.

These loans typically have a slightly higher interest rate than conventional loans, and they often are shorter term, with a balloon payment after two or five years. But they allow investors to purchase, renovate, and hold properties they otherwise might not be able to afford, as portfolio lenders sometimes have lower borrowing requirements than other lenders.

The most common borrower for portfolio loans are house flippers and landlords, so these are the investors who are most impacted when portfolio loans go away. Because conventional loans can't easily be used for flipping, portfolio loans are often the best option. And because portfolio lenders typically don't have a limit on the number of units they'll lend against for an individual landlord, these loans are more flexible than conventional loans for landlords who want to acquire a large portfolio of properties.

Keep in mind that because wholesalers rely on house flippers and landlords to buy their deals, wholesalers are also impacted by the lack of availability of portfolio loans.

Some portfolio lenders specialize in funding multifamily deals, so when these loans are difficult to get, many multifamily investors will find that they have few other options and their businesses will suffer as well.

Finally, because portfolio loans are a great, low-cost option for many small investors, the availability of these types of loans will have an impact on hard-money lenders. When hard-money lenders have to compete with portfolio lenders, they are required to lower their interest rates to be competitive. But, when portfolio lenders aren't lending, hard-money lenders have the ability to raise rates and generate larger profits with less risk.

How does portfolio lending get impacted throughout the cycle?
During the expansion, small banks love to lend to investors. They're lending on flips and rentals, and their interest rates and terms are competitive with conventional lenders. A typical portfolio lender will lend up to 65-75 percent of the costs on a flip and 65 percent of After Repair Value on a rental, and the financial requirements for borrowers are typically pretty reasonable.

As we get toward the top of cycle and over the hump, things change quickly. Unlike conventional lenders who start to require larger down payments and better credit, portfolio lenders just stop lending altogether. The first to go are flip loans. And while some portfolio lenders will continue making loans to landlords, if the downturn is bad, these banks risk running into issues with the FDIC and may have to stop lending altogether. We saw this in 2008 and 2009, when many small banks got shut down by the FDIC, and many others came close.

Keep in mind, this isn't bad for everyone. Hard-money lenders won't see much competition from conventional or portfolio lenders during the downturn, so they have a lot of potential customers who are willing to pay high rates if it means being able to get financing for their flips and rentals.

The tightened lending from portfolio lenders will continue throughout the recession and even throughout the recovery. Late in the recovery, small banks will get their appetite for rental financing back, but many of them won't start lending to house flippers again until the next Expansion Phase. In fact, after the Great Recession, many small banks never resumed lending to house flippers.

Hard-Money Lenders

Hard-money lenders are individuals and companies who specialize in lending to real estate investors. These lenders may be lending their own money or they may be raising money and then lending that money out for a higher rate than they're paying, keeping the difference as their profit.

Hard-money lenders typically have much higher interest rates and less favorable terms than conventional or portfolio lenders, as they care less about the ability for the borrower to repay the loan. These lenders are making their loans in large part based on the value of the real estate asset securing the loan; if the borrower defaults, the lender expects that the property should have a high enough value that it can be sold and the lender can be made whole.

Hard-money lenders are often present at real estate meetups, conferences, and investor association meetings. While there are some hard-money lenders who lend nationally, most lend in a specific geographic region.

House flippers and landlords are the primary customers for hard-money lenders, so they are the investors who benefit when hard-money loans are available and interest rates are relatively low. They are also the ones who suffer when this type of lending is hard to come by or rates are high.

How does hard-money lending get impacted throughout the cycle?
Hard-money lenders have it better throughout the cycle than flippers and landlords. Hard-money lending can work at any point throughout the cycle, presuming the lender has access to funds. Many professional lenders get the money they lend from hedge funds or private investors, and if those sources dry up, so do they. But if they can keep their funds flowing, they can keep lending.

That said, while they'll keep lending, their rates, terms, and requirements will change throughout the cycle. During the expansion, when interest rates are low and there's a lot of competition from all other sources of financing, professional lenders will drop rates and improve their terms to compete with these other sources. But as soon as the market turns and their competition goes away, it's not uncommon to see hard-money rates jump into the mid-teens, including high fees on the front end of the loan. Keep in mind that lenders aren't just trying to take advantage of investors during this time; they have significantly higher risk of getting burned by investors who lose money and don't repay. The high rates compensate them for that risk, something we'll discuss later in the book.

Generally, hard-money lenders will keep their rates high throughout the downturn and the recovery, until other forms of financing start competing with them again, which won't be until the Expansion Phase gets underway. Long story short, hard-money loans are a great backup plan for house flippers and landlords who need money, but throughout most of the cycle, they are an expensive alternative to other forms of lending.

Of course, if you're a hard-money lender and you can get access to funds to lend, you are going to have a strong business model throughout most of the cycle.

Private Lenders

Private lenders are people we know—friends, family, and professional acquaintances. These are generally people who have extra funds in a savings or retirement account and are looking for a better return than what they're currently getting. They lend based on the relationship they have with the investor or borrower, not so much based on the borrower's financing resume or the specific deal. In fact, many private lenders aren't real estate savvy.

Because private money is coming from people we know and who trust us, this type of financing will tend to be cheaper than hard money, and the hoops that investors will have to jump through to acquire this type of financing will generally be very low. Many investors have friends and family who will lend them money quickly and with little due diligence, and in an industry where being able to perform quickly is important, private money is a great option for small investors.

In fact, I know many flippers who rely almost solely on private money for their deals. Some of them can't qualify for portfolio loans or don't have a portfolio lender who serves their area. Others have thin deals that can't afford the high costs and rates associated with funding from a hard-money lender. And others have flipping businesses that require quick closing, and the investors can't afford to spend weeks or months going through the underwriting process with a bank.

Because of this reliance on private money, many house flippers see their businesses grind to a halt when private money dries up and isn't readily available.

Likewise, many other types of investors who can't get traditional financing for their deals will often rely on private money. Note investors rely on private money; land buyers rely on private money; investors who put together creative financing deals rely on private money. These tend to be all-cash businesses, and there aren't any traditional loan products to support these types of investments.

When private money isn't flowing freely, many of these investors will either have to change their strategies or sit on the sidelines, waiting for the private money spigot to turn on again.

The investors who won't suffer when private money isn't readily available are hard-money lenders. Again, hard-money lenders charge higher rates than most other lenders, and when investors have alternatives to hard money, they'll go with those alternatives. When investors don't have alternatives—for example, when private money dries up—hard-money lenders will find themselves with more customers and able to charge higher rates.

How does private lending get impacted throughout the cycle?
This one is easy. Private money is money lent by typical Americans—friends, family, and acquaintances. They'll lend when the economy is strong, when they are confident that their nest eggs are safe, when they have extra money

to invest, and when they aren't worried about their financial situation. In other words, private money is going to flow freely throughout the Expansion Phase, and maybe even into the Peak Phase.

But throughout the rest of the cycle, private money is often not available in any way, shape, or form. Unless you have close family or friends with lots of extra cash, a high tolerance for risk, and a lot of faith in your ability to invest wisely, it's generally safe to assume that you won't have access to any form of private money during any part of the economic cycle other than the Expansion Phase.

Passive Investors

Passive investors are those who invest in syndicated and group-funded deals. We talked about syndications earlier—many large multifamily investors will bring together a group of investors with money and create a partnership that benefits everyone. The person running the syndication is doing all the work and those investing money are just putting up the cash and collecting returns. They are purely passive investors.

When these passive investors no longer want or need to invest in these types of deals, the syndicators lose their livelihood. These are deals that typically cost millions of dollars, and if the person putting the deal together can't find passive investors, they won't be able to do any deals.

How does passing investing get impacted throughout the cycle?

Passive investors are much like private lenders. Economic sentiment is going to play a huge factor in whether they are comfortable in deploying funds for real estate deals. While passive investors are going to be a little bit more comfortable investing during the non-expansion parts of the cycle, don't expect this money to be flowing freely. Also expect that any passive investors you can find during the contraction or recovery parts of the cycle will be looking for higher returns to compensate for the higher risk.

Crowdfunding

Crowdfunding is a relatively new form of financing that's come along with the internet—it's where investors raise money from average people who are looking to invest small sums of money into real estate deals with lots of other people. Crowdfunding companies will help these small investors invest as little as $5,000 into big deals, and the investors will either get interest on their investments or they will become partners in the deal, getting a percentage of the profits.

Most crowdfunding these days is focused on helping flippers and multi-family investors raise money.

Because crowdfunding only started in earnest a few years ago, we don't know how it will change or be impacted by the full economic cycle. I've included it here because it's something we're going to keep an eye on.

Will crowdfunding be recession proof like professional lending? Or will crowdfunding go away during economic turmoil like portfolio lenders?
I guess we'll have to wait until the next economic downturn and see.

CHAPTER 8

INVESTING STRATEGIES

To best leverage the phase of the real estate cycle we're in, we must under-stand and be able to implement a variety of different real estate strategies. While most strategies will work to some degree at any time during the cycle, some are more effective during certain phases than others. To optimize your business at any given time, you need to be flexible and use the strategy that's most effective and profitable—not just one that you happen to like—based on the current market conditions.

If you can only master one strategy because of limited time, knowledge, or capital, there will be times when it will make sense for you to sit on the sidelines and wait for the market to support that particular strategy. There's nothing wrong with this!

Even if you don't have the resources to change strategies as the market fluctuates, understanding the different strategies, and how and when to use them, will give you the knowledge you need to stay out of trouble and take advantage of a great deal if it comes along at an unexpected time.

Strategies versus Tactics

Before we jump into our discussion of the various real estate strategies and how they are affected at different points in the cycle, I wanted to clarify what I mean by the word *strategy*.

We often conflate the terms strategy and tactics, using them interchangeably within our business. But, they are two very different things and I'd be doing you a disservice not to treat them separately.

Strategies are plans of action. These are the high-level things we do in our business to generate income. In real estate, strategies are things like flipping houses, wholesaling, buy and hold, and lending. These are areas that are defined broadly enough to allow us to focus our efforts, without defining exactly how we will achieve success from day to day.

Tactics are the implementations of our strategies. For example, if our strategy was buy and hold, the specific tactics we'd employ might include buying duplexes in blue-collar neighborhoods, financed through portfolio lenders, and held for three to five years. This would be a specific implementation of the higher-level strategy of buy and hold.

In this chapter, I want to discuss the most common real estate strategies and how they will be affected during each phase of the cycle. While it might be tempting to just jump to the section on whatever strategy you're most interested in, consider that the entire purpose of this book is to encourage you to change strategies—and tactics—through the cycle, based on what will work best.

We'll find in this chapter that many real estate strategies will work throughout more than one phase of the cycle. Some even work throughout all phases. But that doesn't mean they will work using the same tactics. In many cases, strategies only work across phases when we modify the tactics we use to implement those strategies.

This will be the focus of the four remaining chapters, where we will discuss each phase in detail, including what tactics will and won't work during each phase.

Common Real Estate Strategies

Please remember that not every cycle—or every phase within a cycle—is going to be the same as previous ones, so it's possible that some of the things I point out here may not hold true during a specific period of time.

This is the reason I have spent so much time focusing on the underlying concepts behind the economy and cycles; I'm hopeful that you now have the information you need to assess the current cycle and make your own determination of whether the information I'm presenting here may deviate in a specific circumstance.

Also note that while I attempt to cover all the major strategies here, there are likely some niche strategies that I don't address specifically. Again, my hope is that the background and concepts I've presented throughout the book have given you the knowledge you'd require to figure out how other strategies may be affected throughout the cycle.

Flipping

Flipping is the process of buying property below market value, adding value through renovation and/or repair, and then reselling it for a profit at or above market value. Because flipping requires you to buy low and sell high, the best times to use this strategy are when property values are increasing, which typically occurs during the recovery and expansion phases. If you try to implement a flipping strategy when property values are decreasing, you may find that the dropping values eat through your profit before you're done with the project, leaving you stuck and either breaking even or losing money.

Because flipping typically takes several months to complete from purchase to sale, flippers need to be particularly careful at the top inflection point of the cycle. Flipping at this point in the cycle can be very profitable if your projects are completed before the downturn begins, because values are peaking. But if you don't complete projects before the downturn starts, you could be setting yourself up to lose money if values drop quickly.

Too many flippers refuse to lose even a little bit of money on their deals, so when a market correction happens and they are holding onto property, they often find themselves waiting for the market to recover. They fail to recognize that it can take years for a full recovery, and eventually these investors may find themselves losing a lot of money, time, or both. If you're a flipper and you find yourself in this situation after the market peak, it's better to cut your losses and accept a small loss than to wait for the market to recover and risk more sizeable losses as the months and possibly years drag on.

House flippers have a tremendous opportunity during the Recovery Phase, shortly after a downturn ends. This is a great time to pick up easy deals in locations where it's easier to resell, to find contractors who are eager for work, and to start scaling a flipping business that has the potential to grow throughout the several years of recovery and expansion.

Of all the strategies we'll discuss, flipping is the one that's most affected by the market cycle, which is why it's important for flippers to understand other strategies and either:

1. Transition to another strategy when the market doesn't support flipping;

2. Sit on the sidelines when the market is declining; or
3. Be ultra conservative if you continue to flip near the cycle peak or during the Recession Phase.

Here is an overview of how flipping fits into the economic cycle:

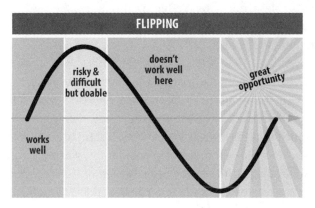

Wholesaling

Wholesaling is the process of finding and/or negotiating the purchase of property below market value and immediately reselling it or the contract to another investor for a profit. Good wholesalers can negotiate prices that are low enough that they can resell for a profit, while allowing their buyer to generate a profit as well.

Wholesalers must buy low and sell high just like flippers. But wholesaling has some additional requirements that must be met for the strategy to be effective:

- Wholesalers most often sell to flippers. So, wholesaling will be most viable during phases of the cycle when flipping is viable.
- The best opportunities for wholesaling exist when deals are exceptionally difficult to find. Otherwise, flippers and landlords will find their own deals without the need for a wholesaler. If you want to implement wholesaling as a strategy, you have to be good at marketing and acquiring property at great prices.
- Wholesalers need to pay even less for properties than flippers because both the wholesaler and the flipper must be able to mark up the price of the property when reselling to make a profit. This can be nearly impossible in both an extremely hot market and a declining market. Great negotiation skills are a major asset for wholesalers.

Like any of the strategies we'll discuss, wholesaling is possible during all parts of the cycle. But because of the additional requirements listed above, it'll be most profitable in a subset of the market conditions where flipping works.

Specifically, wholesaling is most effective during:
- The late part of the Recovery Phase; and
- The Expansion Phase

If you're going to wholesale during other parts of the cycle, it's crucial that you're opportunistic about the properties you buy. Don't expect high volume. Instead, search out the rare great deals. Luckily, wholesalers can position themselves such that they rarely lose money. But trying to wholesale during inopportune times can cost investors considerable wasted time and energy.

Many wholesalers think that the early part of the Recovery Phase is a good time to make money. While it's true that there are a large number of great deals to be had, most of these deals are publicly available, so wholesalers have little value to add. Flippers and landlords can just as easily go onto the MLS and find deals as wholesalers, and they can avoid the wholesaling fee this way as well.

When trying to wholesale during suboptimal parts of the cycle, it's crucial that you have a large network of buyers. Don't just focus on reselling to flippers; also focus on selling to homeowners, landlords, developers, hedge funds, and others, creating additional opportunity during these more difficult times.

Here is an overview of how wholesaling fits into the economic cycle:

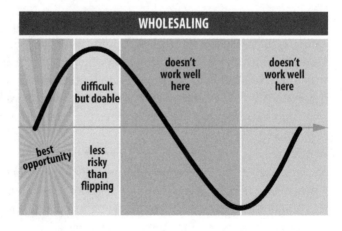

Single-Family, Buy-and-Hold Rentals

Buy and hold involves purchasing a property and renting or leasing it to a tenant who pays for the use of that property. When done properly, the rent paid by the tenant covers all costs associated with holding the property. Plus, hopefully, it generates additional income that becomes the investor's profit.

Like flippers and wholesalers, buy-and-hold investors want to buy low to maximize their earnings, but unlike those other investors, they don't need to sell high. Instead, they want to buy at a price where they can make a profit on the rental income each month, presumably for a long time into the future. So, good buy-and-hold investors are only interested in low purchase prices. For that reason, a buy-and-hold strategy is often best during the recession and recovery phases.

During these two phases, prices tend to be low. Oftentimes homeowners (and even investors) want to get rid of their properties and are willing to sell at a discount. Also, during these phases, there's less competition from flippers and wholesalers, who can often pay more than buy-and-hold investors can afford to pay.

In addition, we frequently see reduced interest rates during the recession and recovery phases, which means lower financing costs if you get loans on your properties. Unfortunately, these lower financing costs come with the additional complexity of getting loans during these periods. Banks often tighten their lending standards during downturns, but if you can qualify for loans, you can often lock in great long-term rates.

Finally, because market rents tend to be lowest during the recession and recovery phases and vacancies tend to be highest, landlords who purchase during these phases will see a bump in profits during other parts of the cycle. Properties that cash flow when purchased during the downturn will generate even greater cash flow when the economy improves, occupancy increases, and rents trend upwards. This is the buy-and-hold equivalent of buying low and selling high (generating cash flow).

While it's certainly possible to continue buying properties during the expansion and peak phases, deals will get more scarce, as house flippers will often be able to pay more for properties than landlords. If you want to continue to buy and hold throughout these phases, expect to work harder to find deals and expect lower returns on those deals.

Finally, ensure that any deals you purchase during the Peak Phase will still generate reasonable returns when we enter the next recession, where rents will likely drop and vacancy will likely rise. We'll discuss this in more detail later.

Here is an overview of how single-family buy and hold fits into the economic cycle:

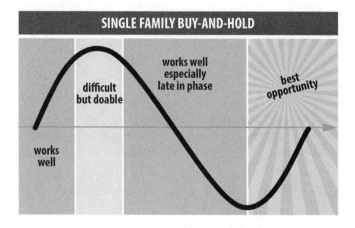

Multifamily

When we talk about multifamily investing, we're typically referring to the purchase of properties with over five units. This could be a small eight-unit residential apartment building, an apartment complex with hundreds of units, or anything in between.

While I talk about multifamily investing as one strategy here, multifamily investing can actually be broken up into two common strategies:

1. **Buying for cash flow.** Cash flow in the multifamily space is essentially the same as buying single-family rentals. The investor is purchasing the property for income well into the future. But these investors prefer to the scale of buying many units at one time and in one place, rather than purchasing single-family houses.

2. **Buying as value-add.** This is the apartment equivalent to flipping single-family houses. When we purchase a single-family home to flip, we are typically buying something that is in bad physical condition, renovating it, and then reselling at a profit based on the physical renovations we've done. In the apartment world, instead of just doing physical renovations, we are improving the financial performance of the property as well. We do this by fixing management, increasing income, and lowering expenses. We can then resell the property at a lower cap rate, which translates to a higher price.

The value-add strategy is often done as part of a syndication, which is a group of passive investors putting money into a project run by the syndicator, an active investor responsible for executing on the deal and earning everyone, including himself, a profit.

Like single-family rentals, buying multifamily properties for cash flow will work during any part of the cycle. And like with single-family properties, this strategy is going to be most successful during the times when it's possible to purchase at low prices.

In the multifamily world, it is cap rates that determines property values, and it's the times when cap rates are high that prices for buyers will be low. This is common when interest rates are high and when sellers are getting desperate to get rid of their properties. Like with single-family, this is going to occur during the Recession Phase (especially the end of the Recession Phase) and during the Recovery Phase.

While it's possible to find good multifamily cash flow deals during the expansion and peak phases, it starts to get more difficult. Interest rates are low, so cap rates are low and prices are high. Additionally, many syndicators are looking to do deals during the expansion and peak phases, so investors buying for cash flow have a good bit more competition.

Value-add typically works best during the Expansion Phase, when cap rates aren't yet too low, rental income is increasing, and vacancies are dropping. Remember, value-add investors make their money by increasing net income, and during an economic expansion, this is happening naturally.

Typically, the value-add process takes about three to five years from purchase to sale, and once cap rates start to rise during the peak and recession phases, value-add investors will find it's more difficult to make money. For this reason, it can be difficult to find good value-add deals during the late part of the Expansion Phase or into the Peak Phase. By the time these deals are ready to be completed, we'll typically be well past the peak and into the downturn.

Here is an overview of how multifamily investing fits into the economic cycle:

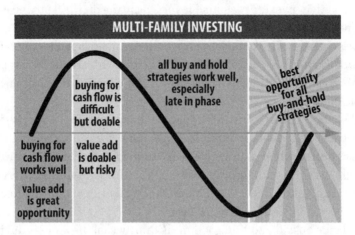

Development/New Construction

Development involves purchasing land, improving it, and either selling it or holding it to generate consistent cash flow. New construction is the process of taking developed land and building on it, or taking a previously developed piece of land, tearing down an existing home, and building on the lot.

Development and new construction can be very lucrative, but these strategies hold the highest risk and are impacted by the market cycle more than other strategies for several reasons:

- Demand for new construction homes is mostly limited to the Expansion Phase and the beginning of the Peak Phase;
- When the market hits the top inflection point, buyers flee from new construction first, often leaving developers and builders with partially completed inventory;
- The time required to implement development and new construction strategies is long—typically at least six months and often many years. Investors who engage in development and new construction must plan ahead and start building during the recovery or expansion phases, so they have inventory to sell during the late expansion and early peak phases when demand is at its highest.

The most successful developers work throughout all phases of the cycle, other than perhaps during the Recession Phase. They buy cheap land and distressed property while the economy is in turmoil (recession and recovery phases) and prices are down. Then they hold their land until values increase and builders are ready to build or homeowners are willing to pay for new construction (expansion and early peak phases).

Developers must strike early and quickly because development has a longer timeline than some of the other strategies we'll discuss. It's not uncommon for developers to lose money during the Peak Phase, as demand is met and fewer homeowners are looking to buy new construction. Good developers will have made enough money during the Expansion Phase that they can declare success, even if they're still holding undeveloped or partially developed land into the downturn.

When the Expansion Phase is longer than average, developers win because demand continues to increase for a long period of time, and they're able to build and sell more of their inventory. But when the Expansion Phase is shorter than average, developers lose because demand decreases sooner than expected, leaving much of their inventory either unsold or having to be sold at a discount.

Here is an overview of how development and new construction fits into the economic cycle:

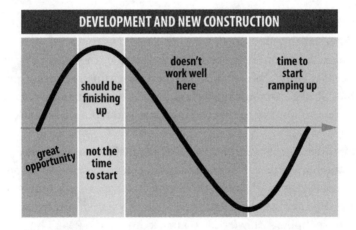

Private and Hard-Money Lending

Private lenders are those who don't lend professionally but who lend to investors. They may be lending to family members, friends, or investors they know and trust. These are individuals who often use money from their retirement accounts to invest in something other than the stock market; or real estate investors who want to diversify their investments by lending to other investors.

Hard-money lenders are typically professional lenders who are securing their loan with the borrower's property, have less of a relationship with the borrower, and are susceptible to risk should the value of the property—their collateral—drop.

Lending can work in any part of the market cycle, especially for those lenders who can underwrite a wide variety of deals. Many successful lenders will diversify their portfolio and lend to different types of investors such as flippers, builders, buy-and-hold landlords, and commercial investors so they can lend regardless of which strategies are working in the current market. If more investors are focused on buy-and-hold deals, good lenders will adjust their strategy to support these types of loans; if investors are focused on new construction, good lenders will figure out a lending strategy that incorporates new construction loans.

But that doesn't mean the phases of the cycle don't impact lenders' profits and margins. They do. Demand impacts lender profits, and interest rates impact lender margins. When interest rates are high, investor demand for money is high, and the supply of loans is low, lending profits and margins will be higher than when interest rates are low and cheap money is readily available.

During the recessionary and recovery phases, when there aren't many professional lenders working and private lenders are scared to deploy their cash, lenders may be able to generate 10 percent or more above bank rates, plus several "points" upfront, on their loans. But during the expansion and peak phases, when lenders are fighting each other to loan money to investors, lenders often have to make loans that rival bank rates, with few fees or points.

Unfortunately, many lenders focus on lending to only one type of investor, such as flippers or buy and hold. And when you lend to only one type of investor, lending will only be viable during the phases of the real estate cycle when that type of investor is making money. Because many private lenders lend to house flippers, they're most at risk during the Peak Phase. Lenders provide loans to flippers need to be especially careful at this point in the cycle, so they don't erase the gains they made during the Expansion Phase.

When we get into the specific tactics to use during each phase of the cycle, we will talk more about how lenders can reduce their risk and optimize their income during the various phases.

Here is an overview of how lending fits into the economic cycle:

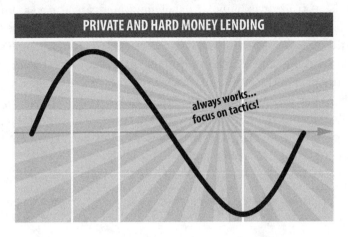

Note Investing

A note is simply a promise to repay a loan (the mortgage agreement you sign is a note), and there are many different strategies around buying, selling, and holding notes.

A few of the most common include:

- Selling property using seller financing and collecting cash flow from the note that's created from the loan;
- Buying "non-performing" notes (notes where the borrower isn't paying as promised) for deep discounts and then working to generate profit from the note by negotiating repayment with the borrower or foreclosing on the property;
- Creating or buying a note, and then selling off parts of a note for quick profit or to borrow against the note.

In addition, investors may purchase notes in either *first position* or as *junior liens*. First position notes are those that are entitled payment first should the borrower default. If the property is foreclosed upon or the borrower is forced to settle debts as part of a bankruptcy, the first position note holders will be the first to get paid. This is a more secure position for most notes.

Junior liens are notes that are not in first position. This means that the note holder is not in first position to be able to foreclose or get paid should the borrower default, and the note holder will typically only see a return if he can convince the borrower to pay or if there is money left over after the first position note holder is repaid their entire balance. If the first position note holder isn't fully paid off, the junior lien holder will typically receive nothing.

This is far from an exhaustive list of how notes can be used as an investment strategy, but I did want to touch on the subject, as notes are often a great strategy during the economic phases where other strategies are less effective. Like lending, notes can be a profitable part of an investment portfolio during any part of the economic cycle, with different strategies providing advantages and disadvantages at different times.

We'll talk more about when to use specific note investing strategies later in the book, but for now, consider that notes are a flexible investment addition to any portfolio and at various points in the cycle.

Here is an overview of how notes fit into the economic cycle:

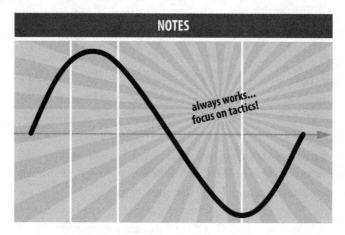

Commercial

Commercial investors invest in various types of real estate other than small residential properties or land (which is sometimes considered commercial investing itself), including:

- Multifamily (apartments)
- Retail space
- Mobile homes
- Office space
- Warehouse space
- Self storage
- And a whole lot more!

Nearly all commercial investing relies on income from regular lease payments, just like in the buy-and-hold strategy. For that reason, the commercial strategy follows many of the same cycle rules as the buy-and-hold strategy.

But there are a few big differences:

- Commercial properties are often much more expensive than single-family, buy-and-hold properties, and commercial lending is typically the tightest during the Recession Phase of the cycle. While commercial investors can often get the best deals during a recession, it's usually the most difficult for them to get the money they need to buy during this phase. Because of that, it's often better to implement a commercial strategy during the recovery and expansion phases when lending requirements start to loosen up and borrowing becomes easier.
- Many commercial investors rely on private investors to fund part or all of their deals. This is a form of investing called private placement or syndication. Because of the reliance on individual investors, commercial investors are most likely to be able to put together these deals during times when smaller individual investors have access to cash and a willingness to risk that cash on a real estate deal.
- Commercial investments often focus on areas that are more recession-resistant than residential property investing, and some commercial investments actually thrive during recessionary periods. For example, self-storage facilities often see a sharp rise in demand during a recession, simply because more families are moving in together or moving into smaller spaces and need a place to store their extra stuff.

While discussing the specific tactics to employ during various parts of the cycle, I'll discuss some of the more common commercial strategies and how they fit into good portfolio management. I encourage you to think creatively about commercial investments and how some less common investments can provide benefits during times when other commercial investments are less profitable.

In general, though, I recommend focusing on the purchase of traditional commercial investments during the recovery and expansion phases. Especially early in the Expansion Phase. And then focus on the purchase of recession-resistant commercial assets as we get closer to the downturn, during the peak and recession phases.

Here is an overview of how commercial investments fit into the economic cycle:

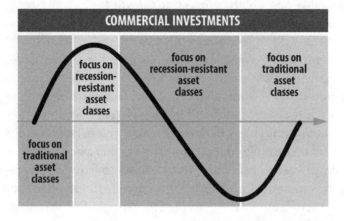

Buying Land

Buying land involves purchasing undeveloped or partially developed parcels with one of several potential exit strategies, the most common being:

1. **Development.** The investor buys land, develops it himself, and either holds it long term or sells it;

2. **Land banking.** The investor buys land and holds onto it, hoping the value increases, and then sells it for a profit to another investor, developer, directly to homeowners, or even to the local government to use for a public development project;

3. **Land flipping/wholesaling.** Some land purchasers are simply looking for an opportunity to buy and resell quickly for a profit, no different than the traditional house flippers and wholesalers we discussed earlier.

If you're buying land to develop it or bank it, the best time to buy is when property values are depressed. When home values are low, land values also tend to be low. This usually happens during the end of the Peak Phase, as the market starts declining and during the Recession Phase when values are falling and investors are looking to cut their losses.

On the other hand, the best time to sell land—if land banking —is during the recovery and expansion phases. Because it takes a long time to develop and build, many developers start to buy land during the Recovery Phase, so they can be prepared for the next expansion. If you own large plots of land, the Recovery Phase can be a good time to sell. At the same time, if you own single lots and smaller plots of land, you can typically hold a bit longer and sell for top dollar to smaller investors interested in building a few houses during the Expansion Phase as demand begins to pick up.

As the Expansion Phase wears on, developers and builders are desperate to buy more land to satisfy demand, and so the value of land increases much more quickly than earlier in the expansion. But holding land toward the end of the Expansion Phase and into the Peak Phase is not without risk. If a downturn comes suddenly and earlier than expected, that land that was appreciating quickly can lose much of its value overnight.

Smart land bankers will "dollar-cost average" as they're buying land, which means they'll purchase at different points in the cycle to average out their portfolio value. And they'll do the same thing when selling, getting rid of their portfolio over time to capture increasing prices but also avoid a catastrophic loss should the market turn before they've sold off a significant percentage of their inventory.

If you're flipping or wholesaling land, the effectiveness of the strategy will generally follow the effectiveness of the flipping and wholesaling strategies. That said, because land flipping often involves lower prices and cash purchases, there tends to be more buyers throughout the cycle, even when financing is tight and money isn't flowing freely. For this reason, good land flippers and wholesalers may have the opportunity to work throughout the entire cycle, especially if they choose their farm areas wisely.

Here is an overview of how land buying fit into the economic cycle:

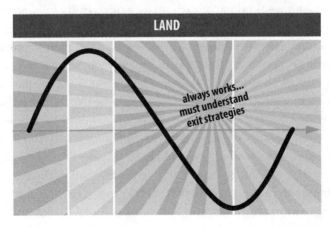

CHAPTER 9

PEAK PHASE

In the next four chapters, we will discuss each phase of the economic cycle individually. Specifically, we'll talk about the signs you can watch out for to determine whether you may be entering or already in a specific phase. We'll discuss how investors can best generate profits and avoid losing money in that phase. And we'll talk about what you can do in that phase to prepare for the next.

That last point is very important. To position yourself for success, you often must start preparing for a specific phase months or even years before it begins. While you shouldn't be spending all your time preparing for the future, we'll discuss the basic steps you can take to get yourself and your business ready.

We're going to start our discussion of the phases with the Peak Phase. This is an arbitrary decision. We could have just as easily started with any of the other phases. But, because I believe that we are in the Peak Phase at the time of this writing, I thought this chapter might be more applicable and interesting to most of my readers.

During the Peak Phase we hit the inflection point at the top of the market. This phase includes both the run-up to the inflection point as well as the downturn just after the inflection point. Unfortunately, we rarely know in the moment when we've reached the top of the market and have started moving down the other side. The turn-around may happen quickly, or the market may plateau for several months, or even a year, before we see an obvious decline.

In fact, it's sometimes difficult even in retrospect to determine when we hit the peak of the market. That's because there may not be a single point of maximum expansion. Instead, we may bounce around the peak, with mixed good and bad economic news over the course of many months, before a clear downward trend begins.

When expansion levels off, there will be people—including prominent economists and financial experts—who sound like Chicken Little, crying that the sky's falling. At the same time, others with just as much credibility will argue that we've simply hit a temporary plateau, after which the upswing will continue for months or years to come. Nobody knows when we've truly hit the peak and trying to time it or predict it is futile.

For this reason, the Peak Phase of the cycle is where the greatest amount of risk lies for most investors. It's in this phase that values begin to drop, occupancy rates start to decline, and rents may decrease in some markets. In some cases, there will be a smooth transition through the peak into the downturn. In other cases, drastic events will throw the market into chaos. A few pieces of bad economic news can create fear that quickly drives the market into a tailspin.

In this chapter, we'll examine some of the signs that indicate we've arrived at this phase in the cycle. We'll talk about how to make money in this phase, and we'll discuss what you can do to prepare for the next phase of the cycle that may not be too far away.

How to Know You're Here

First, it's important to understand that when discussing how we know we've entered a new phase, we need to take into account two types of information: observational clues and quantitative data.

Observational clues are simply the things we notice by looking around, paying attention, and taking in qualitative information. There is no hard data behind these things, but if you're astute, this information is just as valuable as the hard data.

Quantitative data is hard economic data that provides clues on the current status of the economy. Looking at this data and comparing it wtih historic data can provide insight into the state of the economy and how it's changing.

Now, let's jump into how we know when we may have entered the Peak Phase...

In many respects the beginning of the Peak Phase is just a continuation of the Expansion Phase, so there won't necessarily be agreement among investors when we've hit that transition. That said, there are a number of observational clues you can use, as well as some hard economic data.

Observational Clues

Here are some observational clues you can look for to determine when you may be entering the Peak Phase:

- **There's irrational exuberance among the masses**. The economic optimism that characterized the Expansion Phase will transition to an irrational belief that property values, demand, and profits will continue to increase far into the future. Many people—especially those going through their first full investing cycle—will forget the lessons learned during the last recession, and ignore the warning signs that things are more fragile than they appear. In this phase, people often fight over bad investments because they feel like it's impossible to lose money. Many investors are willing to overpay for real estate deals because they're confident property values will continue to rise and by the time they're ready to sell, the increased values will support their purchase price.

- **Money is cheap and easy to obtain.** Private lenders and hard-money lenders are desperate to keep their money working. After all, if they're not lending, they're not seeing profits. Because deals are becoming difficult to find, most lenders have more money to lend than deals to lend on. Private lenders and hard-money lenders alike will be willing to offer great rates and terms, especially to seasoned investors.

- **Banks are offering risky loan products.** It's around this time that banks may start to offer irresponsible loan products like "no doc" loans and 100 percent loan-to-value loans. They've forgotten the lessons from the previous recession and are trying to make as much money as possible during the good times, hoping things will keep chugging along long enough to resell those rancid loans to Wall Street investors.

- **Banks are getting skittish with investor loans.** While banks are offering riskier loans to homeowners, they're getting more conservative with the loans they're making to investors. That's because most homeowner loans get sold off to Wall Street or the government, so the banks have much less risk and exposure with these loans. However, investor loans are more often kept in-house, where banks are at risk should investors default. At this point in the cycle, investors find it hard to get portfolio loans for flips and buy-and-hold properties, and commercial refinances for landlords get harder as well.

- **It's hard to find good deals.** Forget about finding great deals during this part of the cycle; it will become increasingly difficult to find even good ones. Essentially none of the public deals listed on the MLS are suitable for investors, as most homes are selling at or above market value in response to increased demand. There are very few foreclosures. Homeowners don't need to short sale because they have equity. And the quality of deals at public auctions is horrible, as banks aren't willing to give deals on anything. Finding off-market deals is also very difficult during this phase.

- **There are many new, naive investors.** After watching so many others enjoy success from the end of the recovery through the expansion phases, many unseasoned investors decide to join the party thinking there's no way they can lose. But the opposite is true. As many new investors overpay for properties, we once again hear stories of investors losing money.

- **The gurus are out in force.** All the new, naive investors mentioned above have to learn somewhere, so new real estate gurus and coaches are popping up everywhere. Investors you've never heard of are doing infomercials, claiming to have made millions, and offering to reveal their secrets to those willing to fork over large sums of money.

- **Many seasoned investors are moving to the sidelines**. As the number of investors in the market increases, so does competition for deals. While new investors are jumping in and overpaying for property, many seasoned investors recognize the signs of an impending downturn and conserve their cash by slowing down or moving to the sidelines completely. One of the best observational signs that we've moved into the Peak Phase is when investors start complaining that they have more money than they have deals.

Quantitative Data

Here are some quantitative data you can look for to determine when you may be entering the Peak Phase:

- **Interest rates are starting to rise.** As we've discussed several times throughout the book when the economy starts to overheat, and inflation kicks in, the Fed will raise interest rates in response. These interest rate hikes are the first sign from the Fed that they believe things are heating up too quickly and are a good sign that we may be nearing the peak of the cycle.

- **Unemployment rate has leveled off at full employment.** Inflation starts to increase when the economy has hit full employment (generally around 4-5 percent) and business owners have to start paying workers more to fill new positions. It's at this time that we start to see interest rate hikes and a slowdown. When unemployment levels off at between 4-5 percent, we may be entering—or close to entering—the Peak Phase.

- **Cap rates level off and start to rise**. With such high demand during the end of the Expansion Phase, sellers increase their prices, driving down cap rates on income producing properties. Desperate buy-and-hold investors—including large funds and syndicates that have investor funds they need to put to work—purchase deals that generate far less than they would have accepted just a year or two earlier. In some primary and secondary markets, cap rates may drop to within one or two percentage points of current interest rates, especially on bigger multifamily and commercial deals. Around the time cap rates level off at a low point, the Fed is going to start hiking interest rates, which will cause cap rates to tick up.

- **Housing supply hits an inflection point**. Leading up to the top of the market, strong buyer demand creates exceptionally low Days On Market. With prices skyrocketing, homeowners recognize this could be the best and last chance they have to sell their homes for top dollar until the next Peak Phase. As sellers look to cash in on rising prices, new inventory floods the market. At the same time, high prices force many buyers out of the market. With sellers continuing to list and buyers unwilling to buy as readily, inventory and DOM increases in many markets. This DOM reversal is a strong indicator that the market is approaching or has reached the top.

- **Appraisals are coming in lower.** While this one takes many investors by surprise, when the market approaches a peak and banks start going out on a limb with higher-risk loans, they look to mitigate some of their risk by putting pressure on appraisers to keep values from soaring. As the market rushes to the top, investors start to see appraisals both for refinances and resales come in lower than they previously did. Because low appraisals can drive down home values since buyers are often unwilling to purchase at a price above the appraised value, low appraisals can actually contribute to the softening of the market.

- **Profit margins are shrinking for flippers/wholesalers.** Because it's difficult to find deals, flippers and wholesalers spend more of their profits on marketing and acquisition costs. At the same time, competition from other investors drives prices well above where investors can make strong returns. With interest rates rising, inventory levels increase, forcing investors to hold their properties longer. All these things add up to lower profits for flippers and wholesalers.

How to Make Money Here

In this section, we're going to talk about the specific tactics you should be using to make money with the various strategies that work in this phase. In the last chapter, we talked about the difference between strategy and tactics—and we discussed the strategies that we want to employ during each phase. Here we will detail the specific tactics you should be using to execute each of these strategies.

While it's possible to make money during any phase of the economic cycle, all cycles are not equal in terms of risk exposure. In the Peak Phase, there are still plenty of strategies and opportunities to continue making money, but the risk of losing money increases substantially during this phase.

The biggest risk comes from the market changing direction, which causes once profitable investments to lose value. But there are other risks as well. When interest rates rise, profits on cash-flowing assets shrink due to higher borrowing costs. And when your customer base—homeowners, other investors—starts losing their jobs, it's more difficult to sell your properties, lend your capital, and fill your units.

But if you are conservative and employ the right strategies, there are still ways to profit during this part of the market cycle.

- **Flip with caution.** Flipping is still a great strategy, even in this phase. But as you approach the top inflection point, your risk increases significantly. If you're unable to sell your properties before the market starts to decline, you may lose money on your deals. If you're going to flip during the Peak Phase, here are some rules to follow:
  - **Be certain of your numbers.** While it's important to understand the costs you'll incur and the potential profit you could earn in any market phase, it's especially important in a hot market. Knowing and verifying your rehab budget, after repair value (ARV), and fixed costs (buying costs, holding costs, and selling costs) are crucial when the market could level out—or decline—before your project is complete. This is where a great lender can be invaluable. Crowdfunding

providers, hard-money lenders, and private lenders can provide a second set of eyes on your numbers to ensure the deal being funded makes sense.

- **Keep projects quick.** There are parts of the market cycle where taking your time on a project can help you increase your profits. When a market is on an upswing, and it appears that trend will continue for at least another year or two, taking your time means your ARV will likely increase from the beginning to the end of the project. But when you're further into an upswing, the opposite can happen. Dragging out a project won't necessarily result in extra gains, and it may ultimately decrease your profit if the market turns before it's complete. For that reason, if you must choose between a long project with greater profit potential and a quicker-but-less-profitable project, going for the faster project isn't necessarily a bad choice at this point in the cycle.

- **Don't take on more projects than you can work on simultaneously.** In this type of market, I don't recommend buying a lot of properties with the intent of rehabbing them in sequential order (one after the other) because there's a good chance you won't be able to complete all of them before the market turns. In some markets, you may find opportunities to buy multiple properties in a short period of time (for example, the winter months in very cold climates), but that often means not having the manpower to rehab them all at once. While that might be okay in other parts of the cycle, it's not okay during the Peak Phase. If you have properties sitting for months waiting to be rehabbed, you risk having the market turn before you even get started, let alone finished. If you decide to buy multiple properties and you're unable to rehab them at the same time, I highly recommend wholesaling the ones you can't get to or partnering with other investors who have extra bandwidth to take on additional projects.

- **Have multiple exit strategies for each project.** While rehabbers hate to think about what they'll do if a property doesn't sell, in this type of market, it's important to have a plan B, and perhaps a plan C as well. There are plenty of potential exit strategies for rehabbed properties that ultimately can't be flipped. For example, focusing on flips that you're confident would make decent rentals or lease-option properties if you're unable to resell them for a profit can help protect you from sustaining significant losses. You might also consider selling your current home and moving into the rehabbed property until the market improves. There are plenty of backup strategies for flip properties. Just make sure you have at least one or two options in your back pocket when making a purchase during this phase.

- **Avoid thin deals.** While there are times when real estate markets will see a quick and drastic correction (take 2007-08 for example), the shift from upswing to downswing is typically subtler. And often there's a period of time between the upswing and downswing when values stay flat. If you have a deal with returns of 20 percent built into the numbers, the market can drop and you won't lose money on the deal. But when you take on deals with returns of just 5 percent, if the market has even a minor correction, you could be facing potential losses. For that reason, I highly recommend focusing only on deals with relatively large profit margins.

- **Avoid large amounts of leverage.** A lot of rehabbers got into trouble back in 2007-10 because they were getting loans for almost the entire value of the property they were buying (that's what we refer to as large amounts of leverage). That meant if there was even a small correction, the value of the property was less than what the investor owed the lender. And unless the rehabber could come up with some cash to repay the loan, the lender was likely going to foreclose. Rehabbers lost many properties this way in the last real estate recession. If you need to borrow money to finance your flip deals, focus on keeping your loan-to-value ratio (LTV) at no more than 75 percent. That way, even if there's a 25 percent correction in the market, you can still reduce the risk of foreclosure on your properties.

- **Lower your carrying costs.** At this point in the cycle, it's particularly important to keep your costs as low as possible. That way if the market turns before a project is complete, the monthly costs to hold onto it longer term will be less. You'll also have a better chance of recovering your costs and making a profit. There are two ways to do this. First, if possible, pay cash for your properties instead of financing them. Second, if you must finance them, borrow as little as possible to keep your LTV low and pay down your loan as quickly as you can.

- **Focus on properties that appeal to as many potential buyers as possible.** Every market has a "sweet spot" for rehabs—that combination of value, location, house style, and finishing materials—that appeals to the widest range of buyers. When a market shifts into a downswing, these are the types of deals that are the most likely to sell, as there are more potential buyers who may be interested in buying the property when it's listed for sale. When you're in a situation where the market may turn, avoid very low-end rehabs where potential buyers tend to have a more difficult time qualifying for financing. And stay away from exotic or "taste-specific" rehabs that will appeal only to a small segment of the buyer pool.

- **Stay away from high-priced houses.** Higher priced houses will be the first to stop selling when the market turns. As the market declines into a recession, interest rates are typically rising, and wage growth stagnates or declines, which makes it more difficult for consumers to buy a home. If you have a high-end house you're trying to sell, you're going to have a tough time because your buyer pool will be almost non-existent.

- **Avoid speculation unless you're willing to hold long term.** If speculation is part of your investment strategy, be prepared to hold onto your property for longer than usual, and don't buy houses hoping they'll appreciate. Because property values have already been increasing for years at this point in the cycle, you're less likely to be able to turn around, sell a property, and make a profit based on short-term market fluctuations that quickly drive up the property value. It's more likely the value of the property you thought would appreciate either stays flat or declines.

- **Flip in good school districts.** We mentioned above that it's important to focus your flips on properties that will appeal to the largest segment of buyers. In addition, you will want to focus on the houses that tend to be most recession proof. This will include houses in good school districts. These areas tend to be a little bit higher priced, but often attract buyers who have jobs that are more secure during recessionary periods. There tends to be healthy demand for homes in good school districts throughout the cycle, and there also tends to be less competition from homeowners looking to sell their houses in these areas.

- **Buy and hold works but some strategies are better than others.** Like I've mentioned before, buy-and-hold strategies can work throughout any phase of the cycle, but toward the peak, it can be a lot more difficult to find good, cash-flowing deals. Here are tips for how to stay out of trouble when buying for cash flow during this phase and how to maximize your returns:

  - **Assume 10 percent lower market rents.** At this point in the cycle, demand is high, prices are high, and cap rates and returns are low, making it difficult to find good rental deals. More importantly, any buy-and-hold deals at this stage are probably seeing maximum rental income. If you decide to buy to hold during this phase, make sure your purchase analysis factors in the likelihood that rents will drop during the recession—tenants are doubling up, finding lower priced accommodations or even moving back with their parents. This affects market rents, and I like to assume that rents will drop up to 10 percent during the recession. If that doesn't happen in your area, you can consider the extra rental income a bonus above your projections.

- **Assume 10 percent higher vacancy.** Along with a drop in market rents, you should assume there will be higher vacancies after the market declines, and include those factors in your purchase analysis. I like to assume that vacancy will be about 10 percent higher than in the Peak Phase. For example, if you project a 10 percent vacancy for your units during the Peak Phase, you should model an 11 percent vacancy rate during the Recession Phase.

- **Focus on C-class instead of A- or B-class properties.** When the economy tanks, people move from higher-end rentals to less expensive ones to save money. In addition, the largest declines in market rent tend to occur at the higher end of the market. Landlords who are holding C-class properties often do better during recessions than those holding A- and B-class properties, as their income and occupancies will be more resilient to the downturn.

- **Consider student housing.** When the market turns down, full-time college enrollment tends to increase. Higher college enrollment means more demand for student housing. While you should verify the data for the specific location you're considering, student housing may be a great way to purchase buy-and-hold property that increases in value during the downturn as opposed to decreases in value.

- **Multifamily value-add works, but deals are hard to find and there is added risk.** While it's still possible to do multifamily value-add deals, you're likely to find that the bulk of the good deals are gone, and money from passive investors is slowing down. Many investors have already invested in syndications and others are realizing that the market is likely to turn in the near future and are getting skittish about investing in long-term deals at this point in the cycle. I recommend lining up your investment sources prior to looking for deals; you may find that if you come across a decent deal, you won't necessarily be able to raise the funds to purchase it.

- **Change your lending tactics.** If you're a professional or private lender, you should be making changes to your lending strategy to mitigate risk and ensure you're well positioned to make money regardless of when and how severely the market corrects. If you're going to lend during this phase, here are some recommendations:

  - **Increase your interest rates.** If you're lending at this point in the cycle, make sure your rates are high enough to offset the increased risk associated with a potential market correction. Remember, if values drop, the value of any collateral drops as well. If you're holding a note for a $100,000 loan, and the value of the property drops below $100,000, you are now at risk of losing money if the borrower defaults. Because of the desire to keep their money working, many lenders will lend at rates that are probably too low to account for risk at this phase. Don't make that same mistake. Unless your risk threshold is much higher than mine, it's better to make fewer—but more secure — loans than to make more loans, each with more risk.

  - **Lend to landlords before flippers.** As someone who does some private lending, I like to transition my loans away from flip properties and toward landlords at this point in the cycle. Because flip properties only make money at sale and buy-and-hold properties are cash-flowing every month, the risk of lending on flips is significantly higher should the market turn while the loans are still active. When values are dropping, I'd rather have to foreclose on a cash-flowing rental than on a partially completed flip.

  - **Be careful of lending in judicial foreclosure states.** If you're a lender, you always face the possibility of having to foreclose and take back a property from a borrower who doesn't pay. In states that require a judicial process in order to foreclose, you can find yourself tied up in the court system for a year or more waiting for a foreclosure to complete, so you can sell the property and recapture your investment. This is a huge risk if values are likely to fall in that timeframe while waiting for your foreclosure judgment.

- **Note investors should demand discounts.** When borrowers lose their jobs, take pay cuts, and lose access to credit, they are at greater risk of not paying their loans. For this reason, investors who are purchasing notes during the Peak Phase should take some precautions:

- **Beware of purchasing unseasoned notes.** Note seasoning simply means that a note has a proven and consistent track record of payment. A note that is well seasoned has a longer track record of payment than a note that isn't well seasoned. Because borrowers are much more likely to default late in the Peak Phase and into the Recession Phase, it's important to ensure that the notes you're buying have a proven track record of payment. Borrowers who have paid consistently for many years are lower risk to default, simply because they have more equity in their note and they have a track record of success.

- **Look for bigger discounts on notes.** Return is directly correlated to risk—the more risk you anticipate in an investment, the higher return you should demand. Borrowers are much more at risk of defaulting on their notes later in the Peak Phase and into the Recession Phase, so any notes you purchase leading up to that point should be a greater discount. This will provide a higher yield on the purchase of the note, covering the additional risk you'll be taking when purchasing the note.

- **Wholesale instead of flip.** Flipping is inherently risky during the Peak Phase, as the market can reverse and the value of properties in inventory can drop unexpectedly. Wholesalers are more immune to these effects, as they typically don't purchase property and aren't holding property in inventory. I recommend that those who are interested in getting into flipping during this phase consider starting with wholesaling instead. I also recommend that any flippers who want to recession proof their flipping business consider wholesaling at least some of their deals instead of flipping them.

- **Consider recession-resistant commercial assets.** Some real estate assets are more recession resistant than others. And certain commercial investments provide the best opportunity for assets that will likely fare well during a downturn. Specifically, self-storage facilities and mobile home parks are two asset types that tend to not only maintain their income, but see growth, during periods of economic turmoil. If you can pick these up for a reasonable price now, you may find that they are actually worth more once we hit the recession and recovery phases, unlike many other real estate investments. Two other, more niche, recession resistant asset types are grocery-anchored retail shopping centers and medical centers.

- **Avoid short-term borrowing.** Short-term loans for flips or buy-and-hold properties can be extremely attractive, especially during this phase of the cycle, because rates are still low and money is flowing freely. But if the market turns before you've repaid your loan, you may find that the loan comes due prior to completing your exit strategy (sale or refinance), and if you don't have funds in reserve to satisfy the loan, you put yourself at risk of losing the property. In this phase, I highly recommend trying to negotiate loans with longer terms and loan terms that allow you to extend the term of the loan if you haven't completed your exit strategy by the time the loan comes due.
- **Consider using long-term lease options to rent or sell.** If you're having difficulty renting or selling your properties toward the middle or end of this phase, consider using lease options. Lease options give less qualified buyers—for example, someone who can't yet qualify for a mortgage—the opportunity to get into a property, make payments, and hopefully change their financial situation and eventually purchase the property. Not only will you lock in a high price for the property during this phase, but you'll have someone who can help offset your holding costs by paying rent every month.
- **Don't buy land unless you're willing to hold onto it long term.** As I mentioned in the last chapter, the beginning of an expansion is a great time to sell parcels of land to developers who are preparing for the increased demand that typically occurs later in an Expansion Phase. But by the Peak Phase, most developers have already bought all the land they're going to need for the current real estate cycle. The next big opportunity to sell land is likely two to four years off—and prices will drop in that time—so buying land at this point in the cycle is generally going to be suboptimal.

How to Prepare for the Next Phase

As the Peak Phase ends and you approach the beginning of a recession, the market is typically oversaturated with inventory, making it difficult to sell properties. At the same time, cash has been flowing freely for years, leading to an increase in spending and inflation. To temper spending and keep inflation in check, this is the point in the cycle when interest rates typically increase, and lending requirements start to tighten up, making it more difficult for investors to secure the financing to purchase property and continue closing deals.

The Recession Phase is often the most bleak for many investors, especially those who aren't prepared for what's to come. But there are many steps you can take to soften the blow and put you in a position to take advantage of the opportunities that will come available during the downturn and after.

- **Start moving assets to cash.** As interest rates increase and lending requirements tighten, it will become much more difficult to get loans to finance deals. Investors who want to take advantage of great deals during the coming recession will often need cash at their fingertips.

- **Sell anything you're not willing to hold for three to five years.** With values getting ready to drop and interest rates starting to rise, this could be your last best chance to sell off any assets you aren't interested in holding for the next several years. It's tempting to think your returns will be higher if you hold onto the property until the next upswing. And that's often true. But when you factor in the extra risk of holding during a recession and the opportunity cost of not having extra cash available, you may find that selling off a marginal property now is better than waiting years for values to return.

- **Focus on building your credit.** While lending will slow over the next two phases, it won't stop completely. The big difference between borrowing during the Expansion Phase and during the Recession Phase is that banks will require a much stronger financial resume during the recession. A strong credit history can make you more attractive to lenders, and it can take years to shore up your credit if it's filled with dings and negative issues. If you start working on your credit now, you'll find yourself much better positioned to borrow toward the end of the recession and recovery phases when great deals present themselves again.

- **Apply for lines of credit.** When lending requirements get more stringent in the next phase, you'll find that getting loans and credit against your businesses and assets will get more difficult. If you have equity in your personal residence, equity in investment property, or strong personal or business credit, consider taking out lines of credit now as opposed to waiting. The nice thing about most credit lines is that you're not required to borrow against them, and you're only paying interest when and if you do borrow. The downside to qualifying for those credit lines now is low, and the benefits of having access to the cash later could be great.

- **Restructure short-term debt.** Do you have loans that will expire in the next year or two, or will potentially reset at higher interest rates? If so, you may want to restructure that debt now instead of waiting. It will probably be harder to refinance later, and you're likely to receive more favorable terms if you do it now than if you wait. Try to ensure you won't have to refinance any loans you currently have within the next three to five years. And if any of your loans are likely to reset at higher interest rates, attempt to negotiate more favorable terms while you still have some negotiating leverage.

- **Refinance before rates increase.** If you have loans with high interest rates, this could be your last chance to refinance at lower rates. Even a few percentage points can mean the difference between positive and negative cash flow, so work with a trusted banker now to figure out whether refinancing may be worth the upfront cost.

- **Sell off income properties that can't handle a 10 percent decrease in rent or a 10 percent increase in vacancy.** Rental rates in some areas will decrease and vacancy rates are likely to increase. If you can't handle at least a 10 percent decrease in rents and/or a 10 percent increase in vacancies, you should seriously consider selling off the property now to avoid taking larger losses later.

- **Get rid of properties in bad neighborhoods if they're not generating decent cash flow.** As rental rates drop, people look for better houses in better neighborhoods that they can rent for the same monthly rate. You may have difficulty keeping renters in your properties if they're in undesirable locations, so offload them now.

- **Sell anything that can fetch a big premium from speculators.** During the Peak Phase, speculators and desperate investors are overpaying for assets. When the market turns, desperate investors go away and speculators move to the sidelines. If you have properties you can sell for a big profit now, consider doing it to lock in your earnings before values decrease.

- **Cut your losses.** No one wants to lose money on their investments. But if you get caught in a downturn and are holding projects that are going to lose money, it's often better to sell them off for small, quick losses than to hold onto them long term just to break even. The time value of money and stress of holding a property that's underwater generally doesn't make holding on worth it. In fact, one of the biggest mistakes I see investors make during a downturn is not cutting losses soon enough, and finding themselves in a much worse situation later, wishing they'd gotten out sooner.

- **Exercise options when "in the money."** If you have properties or other assets you purchased with an option contract, now's a good time to execute that option if it's in the money, especially if you plan to resell that asset for a profit.

- **Unload rental units you can't rent.** Some condo and townhouse associations limit the number of units they allow owners to rent. During a downturn, more unit owners will decide they need to rent out their units to stay afloat, and you may find yourself competing with them for permission to put a tenant in your property. Find out now if there are rental limits in any of the buildings where you own properties. If there are and you're concerned about not being able to rent those units, sell them now.

- **Consider selling commercial holdings.** If you have commercial buildings—retail or office space—and you don't plan to hold long term, now is a good time to think about selling. When the downturn starts, cap rates will start to rise, and the value of these properties will start to decrease. If you have short-term financing on your property, this is another reason to consider selling, or at least restructuring the debt.

- **Sell FHA properties.** If you own properties you plan to sell to a buyer who will finance their purchase with an FHA loan, don't wait. FHA will likely tighten up its financing rules for some types of properties—especially condos and townhouses—when the market starts to decline. As a result, fewer properties will be FHA-approved, and yours could be one of them. If you don't sell these properties before the downturn, you might be stuck with them until the market recovers. If you're planning to sell, at least check into your condo or townhome association finances to find out if it's likely to be flagged as not FHA-approved.

- **Sell off risky notes.** If you own performing notes where you believe the borrower is likely to run into financial trouble or fall behind on their payments, consider selling off those notes now, even if you have to discount the note. It's better to reduce your profit or take a small loss on a note now than have to foreclose on a property that's underwater and difficult to sell later.

CHAPTER 10

RECESSION PHASE

The Recession Phase of the cycle starts when the economy begins to contract, and many common economic metrics begin to decline. It's characterized by economic turmoil, which frequently includes rising unemployment, higher interest rates, reduced wages, and tightening credit. For real estate investors, the combination of these factors typically leads to a softening of the real estate market, as housing becomes less affordable and financing is more difficult for buyers to obtain.

The government will declare that a downturn is officially a recession after two consecutive quarters of negative GDP growth. But in some cases, the real estate market will take a big hit prior to an official recession being declared. Instead of focusing on how the downturn is formally characterized, I recommend focusing on what's going on in your market, in larger markets, and across the country.

In this chapter we'll examine some of the signs that indicate we've entered a recession and what you can do to keep your business profitable during this phase. Then we'll discuss how you can prepare for the bottom of the market and the coming recovery.

How to Know You're Here

When trying to determine whether we've entered the Recession Phase, there will be a lot more quantitative data to support our conclusion. While the Peak Phase was all about observation, the Recession Phase is mostly about hard economic numbers.

Observational Clues

Here are some observational clues you can look for to determine when you may be entering the Recession Phase:

- **Desperation selling is increasing.** Many homeowners and investors are afraid things will get even worse, so they sell their properties at a big discount to get rid of them before the market declines even further. During the expansion and peak phases, sale prices for similar homes in an area are about the same. However, as we get into the Recession Phase, homes that are similar will have larger pricing disparities because some sellers are more desperate than others.

- **Banks tighten their lending requirements.** When the economy weakens, banks become more concerned about a borrower's ability to repay a loan. As a result, they become more stringent in their lending requirement. Most notably, it's more difficult to find loans for investment properties, especially from small banks, because many lenders aren't willing to accept the increased risk.

- **Few investors remain.** Most of the investors who flooded the market during the expansion and peak phases exit the market during the recession. Investor associations have small turnouts at meetings, and there isn't much investor competition for the properties that are available. The only investors left in the market are those who know how to leverage these new economic conditions.

Quantitative Data

Here is some quantitative data you can look for to determine when you may be entering the Recession Phase:

- **We have two successive quarters of negative GDP.** This is the metric that the U.S. government uses to determine when the country has entered into a recession. While we may be seeing indications of the recession prior to the government making the determination, once there is public recognition that the government has declared a recession, consumer and business owners will start behaving differently with their money, and the downturn will be exacerbated.

- **Housing supply is increasing above the average**. At the beginning of the downturn, interest rates increase and affordability of housing decreases, which together drives increased housing inventory and a softer real estate market. As we move into the recession, rising unemployment and lower wage growth mean fewer buyers will be able to purchase property. And sellers who were on the fence about selling will desperately list their properties, creating a surplus in housing supply. Average days on market for houses will rise quickly, moving from lower-than-historical averages to higher-than-historical averages—about six months in most areas. Later in the Recession Phase, sellers who have financial difficulties will lose their properties to foreclosure, adding even more to the excess inventory and higher days on market in many areas.
- **There's an increase in 30-, 60-, and 90-day late payers.** As broader economic factors deteriorate, and the average American starts to feel the impact, the number of homeowners who are behind on their mortgages starts to rise and continue increasing throughout the recession. Prior to foreclosure rates spiking, we'll see a sharp increase in the number of homeowners who are one to three months behind on their mortgages.
- **There's an increase in foreclosures.** In 2006, prior to the last recession, foreclosure rates across the country were about 0.58 percent; fewer than one out of 150 homeowners were facing foreclosure. By 2010, the height of the Great Recession, that percentage had grown to 2.23 percent; more than one in 50 homes were in foreclosure. One of the most reliable indicators of how far into a recession we are—and when we're coming out of it—is the national foreclosure metric.
- **Home prices are falling.** With an oversupply of houses on the market and a reduction in demand—buyers are losing their jobs, seeing wage contraction, and are having difficulty getting loans — home values decline. When we move from a price leveling off to significant drops in home values, we have entered a recessionary period.
- **Appraisals are coming in low.** During the Peak Phase, we started to see some purchase and refinance appraisals coming in low. Once we hit the Recession Phase, this becomes more acute and a larger percentage of appraisals come in below the contracted sale price. Unfortunately, this is a self-reinforcing situation. When an appraisal comes in low for one house, it reduces the value of any properties that use the house as a comp in the future. Low appraisals drive home values down even more than if they were based strictly on supply and demand.

- **There's an oversupply of new construction.** During this phase, demand for new construction declines significantly, creating an oversupply of inventory on the market. As a result, new construction stalls, and home builders who started new projects during the Peak Phase abandon them because very few new homes are selling. It's better for them to cut their losses instead of investing more money in inventory that likely won't sell. But the result is a landscape of half-completed houses and subdivisions, especially in primary and secondary markets.
- **Rental rates decline and vacancies increase.** Unemployment increases and wage growth decreases during a recession. Renters who lose their jobs or experience a pay cut often seek alternate living arrangements such as moving in with roommates or living with family, which drives down the demand for rentals in many areas. At the same time, homeowners who are unable to sell their properties rent them out in higher volumes than they do during other phases of the real estate cycle. Homes that are newly converted rentals compete with traditional rental properties, creating a larger supply of rentals available, which leads to a decline in rental rates and an increase in vacancies. This won't happen in every market, but in most markets, there will be at least a moderate drop in rents and a moderate rise in vacancy rates.

How to Make Money Here

With fewer investors competing for property, you'll face less competition during this phase. But as the economy continues to weaken, investors face new challenges and risks.

Here are some ways you can maximize profits by investing during this phase of the cycle.

- **Be opportunistic.** Remember, the market will continue to deteriorate as the recession drags on, and there will be some great deals scattered throughout the Recession Phase. Many investors will be tempted to sit on the sidelines and wait for the carnage to end. But the best investors recognize there are some great deals available from desperate sellers throughout this phase, and they will be opportunistic in finding and pouncing on these deals.
- **Buy and hold in good school districts.** The ideal properties for landlords are those in good school districts. They tend to have higher-than-average market rents, lower vacancy rates, and attract better tenants. But these properties are typically priced too high to generate reasonable cash flow

and returns. During the Recession Phase, these properties are often deeply discounted, and this may be your only opportunity to pick properties in great locations at prices that make sense.

- **Start a turnkey rental business.** One great recession-proof business model is turnkey rentals. Turnkey rentals are properties that you purchase, renovate for rent, and then sell for a profit to an investor who is looking for a ready-to-go, cash-flowing property. Many turnkey investors will also place tenants in the property and manage it for an ongoing fee—hence the name "turnkey."
- **Start looking out for early REO deals.** As the recession continues, foreclosures that are working their way through the system will start hitting the market. Depending on how bad the recession is, banks may be discounting these properties heavily, and there may be some great opportunities with little competition. If you're a landlord looking for cash flow, this could be an effective way to start building your portfolio again after waiting out the latter parts of the expansion phase and peak phase. The later we get in the Recession Phase, the more REO deals we'll see hit the market. This is a good opportunity to build a buy-and-hold portfolio, and potentially start buying flip deals when you're confident the market will support a resale.
- **Buy and rehabilitate non-performing notes.** At this point in the cycle, there are many notes where the borrower has either fallen behind on payments or stopped paying altogether. You may be able to purchase these notes for pennies on the dollar, providing you equity in the note and/or allowing you the opportunity to negotiate better terms with the borrower.
- **Wholesale to landlords.** If you're a wholesaler looking to make some money during the Recession Phase, you should be looking to landlords who are interested in taking advantage of down market, but aren't interested in finding and/or negotiating their own deals. While deals should be relatively easy to find—especially later in this phase—many landlords are happy to pay a small fee not to have to deal with the acquisition side of the business. This is where wholesalers come in.
- **Start looking for short-sale deals.** There won't be as many short-sale deals in this phase as the next one, but there will be some. Depending on the severity of the recession, banks may be willing to let homeowners sell for far below the amounts they owe on their mortgages. Because short sales are generally move-in ready, this is an opportunity to start picking up turnkey rentals, either for yourself or to wholesale to buy-and-hold investors.

- **Consider raw land.** If you have the cash and are willing to hold for a few years, now is a good time to buy raw land in areas where new construction has recently stopped. During a recession, many developers give up on the current real estate cycle and stop building. If you buy land from developers now (or banks who have taken back the undeveloped land), you'll likely get a good deal. But you need to be willing to hold onto it (and pay taxes on it) until the next cycle when developers are buying up land again in preparation for the next boom. If you buy from a developer, you may even have an opportunity to sell it back to the same developer in another year or two!

- **Take advantage of seller financing.** Over one-third of all property in the United States is owned free and clear, without any mortgage. And there are always sellers who are desperate to sell for reasons other than financial distress—for example, sellers who are going through a divorce, moving out of state, or selling the house of a deceased relative. For homeowners who own their homes outright but need to sell quickly, this is the time they're most likely to consider seller financing for part of, or all, of the sale price.

- **Purchase with lease options.** Purchasing with lease options is a great way to give yourself the flexibility to control a property while still giving you a future "out" if the recession has a bigger impact on the deal than you anticipated. The benefit to sellers is that they get an upfront option fee, plus they receive a guaranteed monthly income stream until you decide to purchase the property outright or give it back. During a financial crisis, many tired landlords will be happy to turn over control of their properties in this fashion, providing astute investors a great opportunity.

- **Get familiar with subject to and wrap deals.** We discussed using seller financing and lease options previously. These are two common methods of creatively financing your deals. But they aren't the only methods. Two other less common methods can be used very effectively in this phase as well. Subject to involves taking over the payments for a homeowner. The buyer agrees to continue paying the loan as scheduled, and in return, gets the deed from the seller. A wrap is similar to a Subject to, except in this case, the buyer and seller execute a new mortgage agreement that "wraps" the original. This allows the seller to collect additional monthly payments in addition to the loan payments the buyer agreed to take over. Talk to a good attorney to learn the nuances and potential pitfalls of these creative financing techniques.

- **Focus on creative deals that don't require (much) cash.** I already mentioned several examples, but it's worth saying again: A recession is a great time to be focused on creative real estate deals that allow you to purchase properties with little or no money of your own. These strategies may not only provide deals that require little cash, but also deals that are lower risk than an outright purchase. After the 2008 financial crisis, I know many investors who were able to buy dozens and even hundreds of houses using creative techniques and little of their own capital.

- **Modify your at-risk lease options.** If you previously sold property using lease options, now is a good time to think about whether the buyer is under financial hardship and at risk of defaulting on payments or terminating the lease. If so, consider modifying the terms to better suit the buyer's current situation. For example, you can lower the monthly payment, apply more of the payment to the down payment, or even reduce the price of the property to account for any market correction.

- **Take advantage of those investors who didn't prepare.** During a recession, many investors start to regret their decision not to sell off some or all of their inventory when values were higher. They start to worry that they won't be able to afford to hold their portfolio through the downturn, and they decide they'd rather sell at a big discount now than try to weather the storm. If you have the ability to purchase multiple properties at once, you can often get great deals from stressed out investors looking to rid themselves of their headaches, even if it means selling at a big discount. For example, you may be able to pick up a portfolio of rental properties at a price that allows you to make decent cash flow from an investor who is losing money every month.

- **Focus on the lower—but not lowest—end of the market.** Two things tend to be true during a recession: Prospective buyers aren't buying at the very low end of the market, and they're also not buying at the high end. Low-income families tend to be more affected by a recession and fewer will qualify for financing. In addition, the federal and local programs designed to help lower-income families get into homes will see funding and personnel cuts, reducing this buyer pool even more. At the high end, buyers are more likely to be looking to downsize their home and save money on their mortgage. They aren't looking to buy bigger and more expensive houses. The bulk of qualified buyers are middle class, looking for great deals on properties in decent neighborhoods.

This is where you should be focused if you're wholesaling or flipping at this point in the cycle.

- **Buy from banks and funds that sell in bulk.** Banks have legal requirements to avoid carrying too much debt or too many foreclosed properties on the books at any given time. When the foreclosures start piling up, many banks will package them together and sell them in bulk—at big discounts—to investors who have enough cash to handle the purchase. If you have access to pools of cash—for example, by bringing together several investors—you may have the opportunity to pick up several properties at once at a significant discount.
- **Focus on longer-term deals.** Now is a good time to focus on deals that may not have an immediate payoff but can yield a good profit down the road. For example, you might consider purchasing a run-down, empty warehouse in a good part of town that will have significantly more value later in the cycle when it can be converted to condos or apartments.

How to Prepare for the Next Phase

Hopefully you're still making good money during the recession using the tactics we mentioned above, but a bigger flow of deals is around the corner during the Recovery Phase.

Here are some actions you can take now to position yourself to seize the deals that will become available when the market begins its upward trajectory again.

- **Continue hoarding cash.** When the market begins to recover, there will be more opportunity to land great deals than in any other phase of the cycle. But at the beginning of the recovery, lending requirements will still be tight. You'll have the best opportunity to take advantage of the deals that are available if you can pay cash or finance very little of your purchase.
- **Get your real estate license.** A lot of foreclosures and short sales will come available on the MLS as the recession turns into a recovery. Competition for these properties will grow fierce as the recovery progresses, and having direct access to the MLS will give you an advantage over your investor competition.
- **Build relationships with small banks.** Small banks are probably not lending on investment deals at this point in the cycle, but they will start lending again in the next phase. And they prefer to lend to those

they have an existing relationship with. Figure out which small banks were providing investor loans in the previous parts of the cycle, and start building relationships with them. Introduce yourself to the VP of commercial lending. Take them to lunch. Open an account at a local branch. Take out a small loan. Do whatever you need to do to establish a relationship and get yourself known. Additionally, these banks will have their own REO inventory, and may be able to provide a pipeline of deals—and financing for those deals—to their valued customers.

- **Get familiar with the public auction process in your county.** As the recession turns into a recovery, foreclosures will peak, and lots of great deals will present themselves at your local courthouse. The process for buying at the courthouse is different in every jurisdiction, so take some time to get familiar with the process in your area. Start attending some auctions to prepare yourself for the coming onslaught of good deals.
- **Build relationships with lenders, investors, and people with cash.** If you don't have access to lots of cash, there's another option. You can build relationships with other investors who can partner with you on deals and people with cash who are willing to lend or partner. Having money partners will cost you some of your profits, but it will position you to close deals during a time when bank lending is tight.
- **Continue building your credit.** There will be great opportunities for investors to cash in as the real estate market and overall economy improves. But lenders will be cautious about who they loan money to. Continue building your credit now so you'll be a low risk in the next phase when you need to borrow.
- **Start building relationships with contractors, especially if you're a flipper.** As foreclosures and short-sale deals increase, you'll need to be prepared to fix them up and resell them. If you already have relationships with contractors, it'll be much easier to maximize your profits because you'll be able to keep your projects on track, flip them quickly, and move on to the next one. Having a network of contractors you can rely on will help you grow and scale in the next phase.

CHAPTER 11

RECOVERY PHASE

Using the criteria of the U.S. National Bureau of Economic Research, the official arbiter of U.S. recessions, the recession phase has officially ended, and we're moving into the recovery.

Interest rates may still be high, and housing demand is typically still low. But the bleeding has stopped, people are finding work again, and the economy is improving. The government has likely lowered interest rates to spur economic growth, and as the recovery gains momentum and confidence in the economy grows, housing demand increases, and values start to rise again.

That's assuming we've actually hit the bottom. Keep in mind, like we discussed with the inflection point in the Peak Phase, it's possible that we'll bounce along the bottom for a while. We may also experience a "dead cat bounce"—a temporary recovery that looks promising but ultimately drops back to the bottom or below.

Just like at the peak, it's only in retrospect that we'll know we were definitely at the lowest point from where we had nowhere to go but up. But there are some indications we're past this low point, and once we are comfortable that we've hit bottom and are on the road to recovery, there are a number of viable strategies to continue making money.

How to Know You're Here

We won't know for certain that we're in the Recovery Phase until we have a few months of consistent improvements, but there are some indicators that will help you determine if that's the case. Because we're at an inflection point, many of those indicators will be quantitative; but since we may bump along the bottom for a while, it's important to keep your eyes on the observational clues as well.

Observational Clues

Here are some observational clues you can look for to determine when you may be entering the Recovery Phase:

- **Experienced investors are coming off the sidelines.** Those investors who've gone through at least one economic cycle look forward to the opportunities coming available in this phase and have waited and watched for the bottom. When they start to invest again, it's a good indication they believe we've entered the Recovery Phase.
- **A bit of confidence is returning the market.** While we won't see excitement in the markets at this point in the cycle, for the first time in many months—or even a year or two—we will start seeing glimpses of consumer confidence. Homeowners have stopped talking about selling out of desperation and may even be talking about buying new homes.

Quantitative Data

Here is some quantitative data you can look for to determine when you may be entering the Recovery Phase:

- **GDP is increasing, and the end of the recession is declared.** This is the metric that the government will use to determine when we have officially emerged from a recession. While we may see changes before this public announcement—or it may take several more months to see changes after the announcement—the fact that the government has indicated the recession is over will have an impact. Consumers will start to gain confidence and the economic machine will start to churn again.
- **Foreclosures are leveling off.** When the foreclosure rate levels off, there is a good chance that we've hit the bottom inflection point and things are starting to improve. In fact, a *declining* foreclosure rate often means that the worst is in the rearview mirror and we're well on our way to recovery.

- **Housing inventory has peaked and is starting to drop.** In some areas, housing inventory is still at a high point in the cycle, but national data indicates that sales are picking up and some of the excess inventory across the country is starting to get absorbed.
- **General economic indicators are starting to improve.** While general economic data may still be a mixed bag, many of the most prominent metrics—unemployment, GDP, wages—will have either leveled off or shown signs of improvement.

How to Make Money Here

There are many ways to make money in this phase but sticking with the basics will produce solid results with less risk and effort than more complex strategies. Because there is less competition in this phase than in the next two, this is an opportunity to profit on easy deals and prepare your business for when times get tougher.

- **Flippers and landlords have a great opportunity.** If you're flipping houses or buying residential rental property, this point in the cycle provides a fantastic opportunity to pick up inexpensive houses listed publicly, right on the MLS. While not risk free—flippers run the risk of having difficulty reselling and landlords run the risk of high vacancies—this phase is a great opportunity for relatively easy deals.
  - **Focus on REOs.** Not only are there plenty of REO deals on the MLS, but small banks are looking to liquidate their foreclosures as well. Stopping into a local small bank and asking to speak with the head of commercial lending can generate some great REO leads.
  - **Focus on short-sale purchases.** Many homeowners are underwater on their mortgages, especially at the beginning of this phase. To minimize their losses, banks allow some of these homeowners to sell their homes for less than what they owe on their mortgage. This can be a good time to buy homes at a low point in their value and either rent them or resell them for a profit when the market improves.
  - **Buy on the courthouse steps.** Before bank foreclosures become publicly listed REOs, they typically go to auction at the local courthouse. Many investors aren't familiar with the public auction process (it can be overwhelming), but if you take the time to learn the local rules for these auctions, it's a great acquisition resource during this phase of the cycle.

- **Scale your business.** If you're investing full time and looking to scale your business, this is the time to do it. Deals are easy to find, contractors are still desperate for work, and real estate agents aren't very busy and have the time to help you. Many investors wait until later in the cycle to start scaling, at which point deals are harder to come by and building a team has gotten more competitive.
- **Stick with quick and easy projects.** Later in the cycle, during the expansion and peak phases, you'll find that that you need to do bigger and more elaborate renovations to differentiate yourself from the competition. But in this phase, easy projects—sometimes called paint-and-carpet rehabs—return nearly the same amount of profit with less risk, lower capital requirements, and not as much work.
- **Focus on good school districts.** During this phase, deals are easy to find, but they can be difficult to sell. For that reason, it's important to focus your efforts on those properties that will be easiest to sell. Houses in good school districts tend to have strong demand throughout the cycle, and with a lot of families relocating for new jobs after the recession has ended, some school districts will be overwhelmed with potential buyers.

- **Take advantage of good prices for multifamily and commercial.** There's a good chance that multifamily or commercial properties are on sale at this point in the cycle, especially early in the recovery. Cap rates are likely still high, there's unlikely to be a lot of competition from other investors, and owners who survived the downturn without losing their properties may be looking for an opportunity to get out. Now is a great time to start building that rental portfolio or taking advantage of good commercial deals before the economy heats up.
- **Start a turnkey rental business.** We mentioned this in the previous Recession Phase chapter, but turnkey rentals are a great business model during the Recovery Phase as well. There are plenty of good deals to be found during this part of the cycle, allowing investors to make a profit on the turnkey resale, while at the same time providing their investor-buyers a property with both equity and cash flow.
- **Buy performing notes at a discount.** At this point in the cycle, performing notes will be selling at closer to face value than non-performing notes, but will still be selling for less than during the expansion and peak phases. And because the economy is improving, borrowers are more likely to pay and the value of the assets securing the note

are likely to increase in the near future, giving you more equity and security in the note.

- **Take advantage of discounted non-performing notes.** If you're a note buyer, non-performing notes are cheap during this phase. Because borrowers are starting to get back on their feet, negotiating a modification is easier than it was in the previous phase. Also, these notes will accrue equity as housing values rise and the value of their collateral goes up, meaning you'll have less risk with these notes if you hold them further down the road.

- **Purchase using lease options.** Now is a great time to try to buy property using a lease option. You can take control of these properties for a small amount of money, and then wait for the market to improve and lending to loosen up before you have to complete the purchase. The other benefit of this strategy is you can lock in a lower purchase price during this phase, and may find yourself with a lot of equity by the time you complete the purchase.

- **Find buyers who are recovering from financial setback.** If your business model is reselling properties, and you have the ability to provide seller financing, consider seeking out potential buyers who have recently gone through a short sale, foreclosure, or bankruptcy. These buyers want to get back into a house but won't be able to qualify for a conventional loan for several years due to the credit hit they took.

- **Take calculated risks.** Are you looking to try something big in real estate? Perhaps scale a flipping or rental business? Perhaps syndicate a deal or raise a pool of money? While I never recommend taking uncalculated risks in any business, if you're looking for a time to take a well-conceived risk, now is it. Because the market is likely to continue improving for the near future, some of your risk will be mitigated simply because value will be rising and new investors entering the market can help you recover from any mistakes you might make.

- **Consider buying for appreciation.** While I almost never recommend a real estate investor purchase a property with the intent of profiting on its appreciation, this is the one point in the cycle where there is a good chance properties purchased today will be worth more in a couple years, even if you don't do much to them. While I'm not necessarily recommending this strategy, if you like the idea of buying low and holding while the market improves, this is the time to do it.

- **Start marketing land you've been banking.** If you're holding land that you plan sell to developers, start marketing it in the Recovery Phase.

How to Prepare for the Next Phase

The transition from Recovery Phase to Expansion Phase is going to be pretty seamless. In fact, most people don't differentiate between the two, as the Expansion Phase is really just a continuation of the recovery.

That said, there are definitely some differences between the beginning of the upswing (Recovery Phase) and the later parts of the upswing (Expansion Phase), so there are a few things you can do to prepare:

- **Get good at analyzing deals.** The Expansion Phase of the cycle is more competitive when it comes to finding deals. In some parts of the country, this extra competition means smaller profit margins than during the Recovery Phase. Good investors respond by doing larger deals and deals with thinner profits, but it's important to be able to mitigate the added risks of these deals by perfecting your analysis techniques.
- **Dig into the rehab process and learn how larger renovations work.** For the flippers out there, the next phase will bring opportunity to make money on larger renovation projects, adding square footage to properties and even doing teardowns and rebuilds. But to mitigate the extra risk that comes with these types of projects, you'll need to learn all the ins and outs of rehabbing, budgeting, scheduling, and managing a crew of contractors. Even if you plan to hire a general contractor, you need to be able to manage *them*.
- **Figure out your systems and processes.** The next phase provides a good bit of opportunity to scale your business. But if you don't do that efficiently, you'll burn out. I've met dozens of investors who tried to take advantage of all the opportunities in the Expansion Phase and ended up leaving the business after a year or two of 80-hour work weeks and endless headaches. Learning how to scale and optimize your business, as well as how to bring in employees and contractors to help you, will go a long way toward helping scale your business without burning out.
- **Become an expert in marketing.** The easy deals you're finding on the MLS during this cycle won't be around forever, and pretty soon you're going to have to ramp up your marketing machine to keep your deal pipeline filled. This is a great time to figure out which marketing techniques you'll want to focus on, as well as learn the best practices associated with those techniques.
- **Build relationships.** Real estate is a relationship business, and that's never more true than when we get into the Expansion Phase and the entire real estate industry is buzzing with more work than there are workers. It's during this time that it can be difficult to find great

contractors, agents, title companies, and lenders who have the time to sit down with you and make introductions. Make those introductions now, so when the time comes that you need to scale your business, you'll have a network of contractors and vendors who already know who you are and are ready to work with you.

CHAPTER 12

EXPANSION PHASE

Many new investors think the Expansion Phase of the cycle is where the most money can be made. They see a hot market and think "gold rush!" And to some extent, that's true.

During this phase of the cycle, property values steadily rise, demand for property is high, interest rates are still relatively low, and borrowing money is easy. Couple that with the fact that there's relatively minimal risk in this part of the cycle, and the Expansion Phase is a great place to be a real estate investor.

If you take advantage of the opportunities available in this phase, you can earn a lot of money. And you can position yourself to be prepared when the Expansion Phase ends and the other parts of the cycle begin.

How to Know You're Here

We transition to an Expansion Phase from the Recovery Phase. However, it's not always clear when recovery ends and expansion begins, as there is no formal economic delineation between these two phases. I separate them because, as a real estate investor, you'll find that the investing landscape is very different during the early parts of the economic recovery than it is during the later parts of the expansion.

Even though we separate the upwards slope of the cycle into two phases—recovery and expansion—we could probably break the Expansion Phase up even more if we wanted to. That's because the Expansion Phase is typically the longest of the economic cycle. It can last many years, and what you see at the beginning of an expansion can differ significantly from what you see at the end.

So how do we know when we're transitioning from the Recovery Phase to the Expansion Phase? Even if you can't put your finger on exactly when we crossed from one phase to the other, there are some obvious signs we've gotten there. Much like the transition from expansion to peak, there will be more observational clues than hard economic data.

Observational Clues

Here are some observational clues you can look for to determine when you may be entering the Expansion Phase:

- **There is general economic optimism.** When the market enters an expansion phase after a recovery, we typically begin to see growth in much of the economy, not just the real estate market. There's a sense of optimism about where the economy is headed and the positive changes to come. Unemployment drops, wage growth is strong, and consumer spending increases.
- **There's more talk about real estate investing and investing in general.** Average consumers and less sophisticated investors are no longer scared about losing money and are excited about the opportunity to start making some deals. More first-time investors jump in to take advantage of increasing demand and property values. Investors flood the market in anticipation of continued increases in demand and property values.
- **It's no longer easy to find great deals.** Because the economy is strong at this point in the cycle, many homes are once again either above water or getting close. Consequently, the number of foreclosures and short sales is lower than it was just a few months earlier and is continuing to decrease. With more investors joining the party, it's not uncommon to find yourself in battles over the limited number of deals that are publicly available through the MLS, public auctions, and other public sales.
- **Off-market strategies gain attention.** More investors start to build acquisition strategies around finding "off-market" deals. Direct-mail campaigns get popular, bandits signs are everywhere (billboards

advertising "We Buy Houses!" are popping up again), and more investors rely on door knocking and cold-calling to find deals.

- **Selling to homeowners is easier**. As demand for housing increases, more homeowners jump off the fence and start looking for good deals on personal residences. At the same time, banks loosen lending requirements, so more homeowners qualify for mortgages.
- **Professional money is easier to find.** Lenders start popping up at REIA meetings, investor conferences, and other places where investors hang out. For the first time in a while, money is easier to acquire than deals, and lenders begin to compete with each other.
- **Private money is easier to find.** Regular people look for places to put their capital. As the economy gets stronger, it's possible to find money from private individuals who have extra cash and are looking to put that money to work. Individuals with self-directed IRAs who are interested in diversifying their investment portfolios are happy to loan money to investors. And others are looking to partner with investors on real estate deals.
- **You're competing with cash offers.** When the economy heats up, the market fills with new and eager investors. As money starts to flow more freely throughout the industry, you'll find that you're competing with cash offers more frequently. Sellers will recognize there are buyers who can and will pay cash for deals, and they start holding out for cash buyers.
- **You're competing with commercial buyers.** Public hedge funds and large private equity funds have a knack for recognizing when the economy is starting to grow. When these firms jump into the market, it's an indication we've hit the Expansion Phase, and they actually play a part in driving the expansion. During the early Expansion Phase, you'll find that you're being outbid by larger private organizations, and you may discover that these organizations are interested in buying your properties.
- **Gurus come out of the woodwork.** For any investors going through their first cycle, you might assume that real estate gurus pitching seminars, courses, and high-priced training are common in the industry at all times. But that's not the case. For much of the cycle, these gurus are investing themselves, taking advantage of the market and making easy money. But, after doing ten, 20, or 100 deals, they realize that real estate investing is *work*. With all the new investors popping up during the Expansion Phase, there's an opportunity to make easy

money teaching and training. When you see and hear about real estate training everywhere you look, there's a good chance we're in the later parts of the Expansion Phase or the Peak Phase.

Quantitative Data

Here is some quantitative data you can look for to determine when you may be entering the Expansion Phase:

- **Housing supply is dropping**. The DOM in most markets is trending down and may be lower than the general average of six months. As demand continues to increase, sellers gain control of the market, and property values increase. You'll hear that it's a seller's market once again and buyers will be paying significantly more for properties than just a few months earlier.
- **Appraisals are coming in higher.** Investors have less difficulty getting their properties to appraise at the contract price when reselling or refinancing. There are more comps for appraisers to use to justify resale values, and banks are less likely to question appraisals because they perceive less risk as values rise.
- **Money is getting cheaper.** Private lenders are once again willing to lend, which puts more pressure on professional lenders, and rates start to drop across the board.

How to Make Money Here

During an economic expansion, most of the investing strategies we discussed in the previous chapter will work to some degree, and the most common strategy—flipping houses—will be in full force across most markets. This is a time during the cycle that represents low risk and high reward for many investing strategies, including flipping, wholesaling, buy and hold, development, lending, and commercial.

Making money during the Expansion Phase is pretty straightforward. Here's how you can take advantage of the opportunities available to you.

- **Scale your flipping and wholesaling efforts.** This is the phase in the cycle where flippers and wholesalers can make a lot of money by scaling their businesses and increasing their volume. Although it will get tougher to find great deals as the economic expansion wears on, there will still be plenty of good deals throughout much of this phase. Focus on finding off-market deals to keep your deal pipeline filled and your team and contracting crews busy.

- **Consider a live-in flip.** One of the greatest benefits of homeownership in the United States is the exemption from capital gains tax (up to certain limits) on profits from the sale of your personal residence. But to qualify for this exemption, you must live in your house for at least two years. Many astute investors take advantage of this tax loophole by moving to a new personal residence every two years. This strategy is especially effective early in the Expansion Phase. If you can purchase a house early in this phase, there's a good chance it will be worth more two years later, allowing you to lock in a tax-free profit. And if the expansion is of average length or more, you should be able to perform this strategy at least twice—and maybe three times—before the market turns.
- **Get good at larger renovations.** If you're a flipper, you'll find that later in this phase there's a lot of competition for the easy renovation projects. The best way to differentiate yourself and keep your pipeline filled with profitable deals will be to buy the properties that require more extensive renovations, adding square footage, raising the roof and adding a second story, or tearing down and rebuilding. Other investors are scared to take on these projects, giving you a competitive advantage through the rest of this phase.
- **Build relationships with the large and institutional buyers.** During the early part of the Expansion Phase, hedge funds and large private equity firms start buying in volume, especially in primary and secondary markets. While these firms often prove to be your competition when looking for deals, they are potentially your customers when selling. If you can build relationships with representatives from these companies, you may find they're looking to buy the types of deals you're selling. Between 2012 and 2014, we sold dozens of deals to hedge funds buying in Atlanta, Georgia, and even built a business model around selling to those buyers.
- **Raise money for syndications and private placements.** Many real estate strategies rely on—or benefit from—raising outside capital. In some cases, investors want to scale their flipping or note business. In other cases, investors want to buy an expensive asset like an apartment complex or mobile home park. Oftentimes, these investors look to private investors to pool capital in what's known as a syndication or private placement. At this point in the economic cycle, smaller investors are once again getting comfortable investing in other people's deals, so it's a great time to raise money. Additionally, because the market isn't

yet overheated, there are plenty of deals available to put that raised capital to work.

- **Get the last of the great buy-and-hold deals.** The most plentiful buy-and-hold deals were in the previous phase, but there should still be plenty of good deals for landlords during the Expansion Phase, especially the early part. Because occupancy rates and market rents will likely increase throughout this phase, anything you buy earlier in the economic expansion should have a good bit of upside when it comes to future revenue. That said, as we approach the tail end of the Expansion Phase, finding good rental deals will be very difficult. Many other investors recognize that this is the last opportunity in this cycle to convert cash to cash flow, and you'll have a lot of competition for the few good deals remaining.

- **Cash-flow through private lending**. Demand for private lending picks up during the Expansion Phase, as many investors want to scale their businesses but don't have access to as much financing as they'd like. If you're lending to other investors, you can expect to get decent interest rates and earn solid returns on your investments. An additional benefit to lending during this phase in the cycle is that market risk is low. If you lend on a property that you later have to take back from the borrower because they default on the loan, there's a good chance you can sell it and get your investment and your return back.

- **Invest in performing notes.** As mentioned earlier, there are opportunities for note investing throughout all phases of the economic cycle. During the Expansion Phase, creating or buying performing notes is a great way to generate consistent cash flow with relatively low risk. A common note strategy during this phase is to sell assets using seller financing (create a note for yourself). As buyers consistently make their payments, the resale value of the note increases, providing the opportunity to sell the note or borrow against it later in the cycle.

- **Sell large parcels of land.** If you've been holding on to large parcels of land that you plan to sell to a developer, the beginning of an expansion is the best time to market it. Because it takes several years to develop and build a parcel, builders generally buy land a couple of years before they plan to resell it. They often purchase it at the beginning of an expansion in anticipation of the increased demand that typically occurs later in the expansion and during the Peak Phase. If the Expansion Phase lasts longer than normal, developers may deplete the inventory of land they bought earlier in the phase and need to buy more. If this happens, you may be able to sell your land for a higher price later in the cycle. But there's no guarantee that will occur, and many developers won't buy land at that point in the cycle because they know the market will eventually turn. If you hold onto your land for too long, you might miss out since you don't know when the decline is going to begin. This could be your last chance to offload your land during this cycle.

- **Take advantage of available commercial deals.** Depending on what's going on with cap rates and interest rates, this may be your last opportunity to snag great commercial deals for a while. Purchase prices are still reasonable at this point in the cycle, while rental rates and occupancy rates will be increasing throughout this phase and into the peak, making it an ideal time to buy. If you're a commercial investor, now's the time to grow your portfolio.

How to Prepare for the Next Phase

With so many factors working in your favor during an expansion, there's less of a question about how to make money than there is about how to continue making money as we enter the Peak Phase.

During the next phase of the cycle—the Peak Phase—investors will flood the market looking to cash in before the downturn. And competition will increase, making it more difficult to find good deals. One of the most important things you can do during the Expansion Phase is watch for signs we're moving into the Peak Phase, so you can react quickly and avoid the consequences of hitting the peak of the market without being prepared for it.

The Peak Phase is generally pretty short. Generating profits in this phase is about flexibility and being opportunistic. Other than watching for it, there's not a whole lot you can do to prepare for this upcoming phase. But I do have some suggestions:

- **Refinance high-interest rate loans.** If you have loans with high interest rates, this may be your last chance to refinance at lower rates. During the Peak Phase, the Fed will likely raise interest rates to combat inflation. Locking in a great rate now can help you generate and protect gains later. In addition to allowing you to generate greater returns on your assets, refinancing helps reduce your interest payments, freeing up extra cash you can use to complete more deals.
- **Shore up your cash-flowing assets.** If you're a buy-and-hold or commercial investor, this could be your last chance to acquire good deals for a while. Instead of just focusing on acquiring more deals, take this

opportunity to capitalize on profits your properties are generating. Maximize income by increasing rents on your existing properties if they're below market value. And figure out where you can streamline your business to decrease expenses. A few dollars in extra profits at this point in the cycle may not mean much, but when the downturn comes, you'll be glad that properties are running efficiently and at maximum profit potential.

- **Fill your units with the right tenants.** Along with maximizing your rental income and minimizing expenses, now's the time to take a hard look at your rent rolls and determine whether you should be turning over problem tenants. Most of your tenants will be able to pay rent on time when the economy is good, but that will change as people are lose their jobs and see wage decreases. If you have tenants who aren't paying on time now or who are causing headaches, consider that they will likely cause bigger issues when the market turns. If you can legally get rid of those tenants now, you should take the opportunity.

- **Perfect marketing and acquisition strategies to build a sustainable pipeline.** As we approach the end of an Expansion Phase and beginning of the Peak Phase, foreclosures and short sales will have dried up. If you're a flipper or wholesaler, acquisition gets very difficult at this point in the cycle. Now's the time to prepare by improving your off-market acquisition strategies including yellow letters, knocking on doors, SEO, advertising, and partnering with wholesalers, because during the next phase you won't be able to rely on public sales. Keep in mind that other investors will be using these same strategies, so be ready for the competition.

FINAL THOUGHTS

While writing this book I had discussions with some investors who I highly respect and admire. One of the recurring themes of those discussions was the idea that great investors should be able to focus on a single strategy throughout the entire market cycle and still be successful.

I don't disagree with this. Those who are world-class at a given investing strategy can use that strategy continuously and are likely to be successful no matter what obstacles the market throws at them. They are so good at the one thing they do they can make money doing it any place, any time, and under any conditions.

But many of us aren't the best in the world at a given strategy. For us, trying to fight the market is an effort in futility; either we don't have the skills to execute on a single strategy at every point in the market cycle or we don't have the desire to try. And for us mere mortals, the idea of bending and flexing to the whims of the market makes a lot more sense than standing up to the market and challenging it to take us down.

Personally, I always prefer the path of least resistance. That mindset, along with the philosophies and strategies I've laid out here, have worked well for me throughout the last business cycle. I hope you'll find they work for you as well.

In the meantime, if you have any additional thoughts, recommendations, or feedback on the information I've provided, don't hesitate to shoot me an email at recessionproof@biggerpockets.com.

—J Scott

GLOSSARY

Appreciation   The increase in the value of an asset over time.

Bonds   Debt (often provided by the government) that pays a fixed interest to the investor.

Business cycle   The cyclical expansion (strong economy) and contraction (weak economy) that we see about once a decade or so, and what we typically think of as basic economic fluctuations.

Buyer's market   Part of the real estate cycle in which there are more houses for sale than people to buy them. A housing market that favors buyers.

Capitalization rate (Cap rate)   The income generated by a property divided by the value of the property. This metric indicates the percentage return an investor could expect by purchasing this property.

DOM   "Days on market." The amount of time a real estate listing has been on the market. Also used to indicate the average amount of time a property in an area can expect to sit before getting a contract.

Expansion   Business cycle phase in which buyer demand for housing is increasing as other economic factors such as wage and job growth are strong.

Federal Reserve (the Fed)   The central bank of the United States. The Fed sets monetary policy for the country, including controlling interest rates by defining the rate at which banks are required to borrow from the government.

Foreclosure   The legal process by which a lender takes back a property from a borrower who isn't paying as promised.

Full employment   Unemployment rate at which most Americans who are looking for work have found jobs. The Federal Reserve considers a base unemployment rate (the U-3 rate) of 5 to 5.2 percent as "full employment" in the economy.

GDP   "Gross domestic product." The total annual economic output by a country.

Housing starts   The number of residential housing units that are beginning the process of being permitted and built.

Housing supply   See "Inventory."

Inflation   A general increase in prices for goods and services.

Inflection points   In an economic cycle, points at the very top and very bottom of the curve.

Interest rate   The cost to borrow money or the return on lending money.

Inventory   The number of months it would take to sell the entire housing inventory currently for sale in an area.

Judicial foreclosure   A foreclosure that is required to go through the court system before being legally granted. Judicial foreclosures tend to take much longer than non-judicial foreclosures.

Leading indicators   Economic factors that shift before you see major changes in a specific market or the general economy; precursors to change.

Lease option   A type of purchase contract whereby the owner agrees to allow the buyer to lease a property for a fixed period of time, during which time the buyer has the option to buy the property.

Leverage   The use of borrowed capital to purchase and/or increase the potential return of an investment.

Long-term debt cycle   A longer economic cycle, lasting between 75 and 100 years, where the debt bubble slowly expands and eventually pops.

Non-performing note   A note on which the borrower isn't paying as promised.

Note   A promise to repay a loan; one common example is a mortgage note.

Peak   Business cycle phase in which prices hit a plateau and demand starts to soften.

Performing note   A note on which the borrower is paying as promised.

Points   A percentage of the total loan amount, typically paid as a fee prior to the loan being made. One point equals 1 percent of the loan amount.

Portfolio loans   Loan products with different requirements than offered by government entities. These loans are generally offered by smaller banks to investors, typically in a strong economy when the risk of borrowers defaulting on real estate loans is low.

Private placement   An investing fund created by raising money from smaller, individual investors.

Profit margins   The percentage of the total revenue earned by a business kept as profit.

Recession   Business cycle phase in which there is general economic turmoil; some common elements include high unemployment, reduced wages, and tightening of credit.

Recovery   Business cycle phase where economy starts to recover after hitting bottom.

REO   "Real estate owned." An industry term for a bank-owned foreclosure.

ROI   Return on investment.

Seller financing   Creative financing method by which the seller of a property uses equity in the property to provide a loan to a buyer.

Seller's market   Part of the real estate cycle in which more people want to buy houses than want to sell them. A housing market that favors sellers.

Subject to   Creative financing method by which the buyer of a property takes over the payments of the seller's loan in return for possession and deed of the house.

Syndication   A form of investing relying on the combined funds of several private investors who have pooled capital to fund part or all of a deal.

Trailing indicators   Economic metrics seen as a result of shifts in a market or economy; successors to change.

Underwrite   The process that a lender uses to assess the creditworthiness or risk of a potential customer and/or loan collateral.

Wrap   Creative financing method by which the seller and buyer create a new loan that requires the buyer to pay the sellers existing loan, plus allows the seller to collect additional payments.

Yield curve   The change in interest rates for government bonds of different expiration dates.

NOTES

Chapter 5

1. U.S. Bureau of Labor Statistics, Civilian Unemployment Rate [UNRATE], retrieved from FRED, Federal Reserve Bank of St. Louis; https://fred.stlouisfed.org/series/UNRATE, June 8, 2022.

2. Wilshire Associates, Wilshire 5000 Total Market Full Cap Index [WILL5000INDFC], FRED, Federal Reserve Bank of St. Louis; https://fred.stlouisfed.org/series/WILL5000INDFC, June 8, 2022.

3. U.S. Bureau of Economic Analysis, Real Gross Domestic Product [A191RL1Q225SBEA], retrieved from FRED, Federal Reserve Bank of St. Louis; https://fred.stlouisfed.org/series/A191RL1Q225SBEA, January 9, 2019.

4. Board of Governors of the Federal Reserve System (U.S.), Effective Federal Funds Rate [FEDFUNDS], retrieved from FRED, Federal Reserve Bank of St. Louis; https://fred.stlouisfed.org/series/FEDFUNDS, June 8, 2022.

5. Organization for Economic Co-operation and Development, Hourly Earnings: Manufacturing for the United States [LCEAMN01USM659S], retrieved from FRED, Federal Reserve Bank of St. Louis; https://fred.stlouisfed.org/series/LCEAMN01USM659S, June 8, 2022.

6. U.S. Bureau of the Census and U.S. Department of Housing and Urban Development, Monthly Supply of Houses in the United States [MSACSR], retrieved from FRED, Federal Reserve Bank of St. Louis; https://fred.stlouisfed.org/series/MSACSR, January 9, 2019.

7. U.S. Bureau of the Census and U.S. Department of Housing and Urban Development, Housing Starts: Total: New Privately Owned Housing

Units Started [HOUST], retrieved from FRED, Federal Reserve Bank of St. Louis; https://fred.stlouisfed.org/series/HOUST, June 8, 2022.

8. U.S. Bureau of the Census and U.S. Department of Housing and Urban Development, Housing Starts: Total: New Privately Owned Housing Units Started [HOUST], retrieved from FRED, Federal Reserve Bank of St. Louis; https://fred.stlouisfed.org/series/HOUST, January 9, 2019.

Chatper 6

9. U.S. Bureau of the Census and U.S. Department of Housing and Urban Development, Monthly Supply of Houses in the United States [MSACSR], retrieved from FRED, Federal Reserve Bank of St. Louis; https://fred.stlouisfed.org/series/MSACSR, June 8, 2022.

ABOUT THE AUTHOR

J Scott (he goes by "J") is an entrepreneur, investor, and the co-host of The BiggerPockets Business Podcast. An engineer and business guy by education, J spent much of his early career in Silicon Valley, where he held management positions at several Fortune 500 companies, including Microsoft and eBay.

In 2008, J and his wife Carol quit their corporate jobs, moved back east, got married, started a family, and decided to focus on real estate and investing. In the past ten years, they have bought, built, rehabbed, sold, lent-on, and held over $50 million in property all around the country.

J is also a business owner, business advisor, and mentor to several companies, business owners, and entrepreneurs.

J runs the popular website 123Flip.com and is the author of four books on real estate investing, including the best-selling, *The Book on Flipping Houses*. His books have sold more than 200,000 copies in the past six years and have helped investors from around the world get their start in real estate.

J and his family currently live in Sarasota, FL. J can be reached at j@jscott.com.

More from
BiggerPockets Publishing

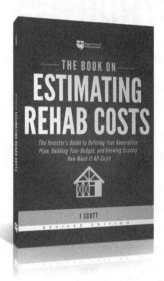

The Book on Estimating Rehab Costs, Revised Edition

Learn detailed tips, tricks, and tactics to accurately budget nearly any house flipping project from expert fix-and-flipper J Scott. Whether you are preparing to walk through your very first rehab project or you're an experienced home flipper, this handbook will be your guide to identifying renovation projects, creating a scope of work, and staying on budget to ensure a timely profit!

The Book on Flipping Houses, Revised Edition

Written by active real estate investor and fix-and-flipper J Scott, this book contains more than 300 pages of step-by-step training, perfect for both the complete newbie and the seasoned pro looking to build a house-flipping business. Whatever your skill level, this book will teach you everything you need to know to build a profitable business and start living the life of your dreams.

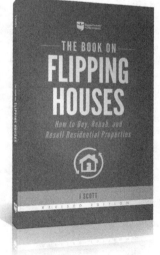

If you enjoyed this book, we hope you'll take a moment to check out some of the other great material BiggerPockets offers. BiggerPockets is the real estate investing social network, marketplace, and information hub, designed to help make you a smarter real estate investor through podcasts, books, blog posts, videos, forums, and more. Sign up today—it's free! **Visit www.BiggerPockets.com.**

Long-Distance Real Estate Investing

Don't let your location dictate your financial freedom: Live where you want, and invest anywhere it makes sense! The rules, technology, and markets have changed: No longer are you forced to invest only in your backyard. In *Long-Distance Real Estate Investing*, learn an in-depth strategy to build profitable rental portfolios through buying, managing, and flipping out-of-state properties from real estate investor and agent David Greene.

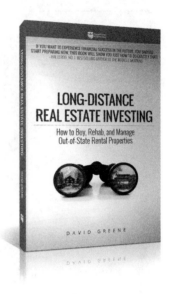

The Book on Investing in Real Estate with No (and Low) Money Down

Is lack of money holding you back from real estate success? It doesn't have to! In this groundbreaking book from Brandon Turner, author of *The Book on Rental Property Investing* and others, you'll discover numerous strategies investors can use to buy real estate using other people's money. You'll learn the top strategies that savvy investors are using to buy, rent, flip, or wholesale properties at scale!

More from
BiggerPockets Publishing

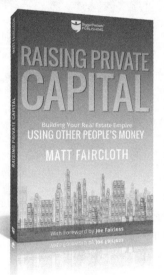

Raising Private Capital

Are you ready to help other investors build their wealth while you build your real estate empire? The road map outlined in *Raising Private Capital* helps investors looking to inject more private capital into their business—the most effective strategy for growth! Author and investor Matt Faircloth helps you learn how to develop long-term wealth from his valuable lessons and experiences in real estate: Get the truth behind the wins and losses from someone who has experienced it all.

The Book on Tax Strategies for the Savvy Real Estate Investor

Taxes! Boring and irritating, right? Perhaps. But if you want to succeed in real estate, your tax strategy will play a huge role in how fast you grow. A great tax strategy can save you thousands of dollars a year. A bad strategy could land you in legal trouble. That's why BiggerPockets is excited to offer *The Book on Tax Strategies for the Savvy Real Estate Investor*! You'll find ways to deduct more, invest smarter, and pay far less to the IRS!

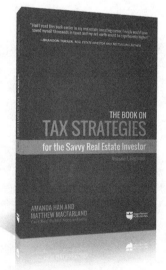

Real Estate Note Investing

Are you a wholesaler, a rehabber, a landlord, or even a turnkey investor? *Real Estate Note Investing* will help you turn your focus to the "other side" of real estate investing, allowing you to make money without tenants, toilets, and termites! Investing in notes is the easiest strategy to make passive income. Learn the ins-and-outs of notes as investor Dave Van Horn shows you how to get started—and find huge success—in the powerful world of real estate notes!

The Book on Rental Property Investing

The Book on Rental Property Investing by Brandon Turner, a real estate investor and cohost of the *BiggerPockets Podcast*, contains nearly 400 pages of in-depth advice and strategies for building wealth through rental properties. You will learn how to build an achievable plan, find incredible deals, pay for your rentals, and much more!

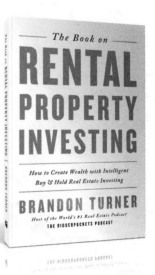

CONNECT WITH BIGGERPOCKETS

and Become Successful in Your Real Estate Business Today!

Facebook
/BiggerPockets

Instagram
@BiggerPockets

Twitter
@BiggerPockets

LinkedIn
/company/Bigger
Pockets

Website
BiggerPockets.com